D1554887

COACHING OFFENSIVE LINE PLAY

Nick Metrokotsas

MacGregor Sports Education
East Rutherford, New Jersey

This book was originally published
under the title *The Complete
Book of Offensive Line Play*

© 1987, 1977, *by*

MacGregor Sports Education

East Rutherford, N.J.

*All rights reserved. No part of this book
may be reproduced in any form or by any
means, without permission in writing from
the publisher.*

Library of Congress Cataloging-in-Publication Data

Metrokotsas, Nick
   Coaching offensive line play.

   1. Football—Offensive. 2. Football—Coaching.
I. Title.
GV951.8M46 1987   796.332'2   87-2607
ISBN 0-941175-00-6

ISBN 0-941175-00-6

Printed in the United States of America

Contents

This book is dedicated to my mother and father, Anita and Nick Metrokotsas, for their support and encouragement during my career as a player and as a coach.

CHAPTER 1

One-On-One Blocking

Since this book teaches all phases of offensive line play, we feel that it is necessary to introduce it with a statement of our coaching philosophy in this area. Simply stated, our philosophy is: "A great block begins with a great stance." It is difficult to imagine how a great block, which depends on quickness, balance, visibility and power, could ever be executed from a stance that did not lend itself to these characteristics. Therefore, we spend a great deal of time with our linemen in order to develop a stance that will permit them to execute their blocking assignments with maximum quickness, perfect balance, 100 percent visibility and tremendous power.

THE PERFECT STANCE

Quickness

In order to insure quickness, three techniques are important. The first and most important is proper weight distribution. The lineman who sits back on his feet can not hope to move quickly straight ahead. Offensive linemen are often called on to pull to either side, fire-out straight, step left or right and set up in pass protection. In any assignment, the blocker must be set in the same stance, a stance that will allow him to move in all directions with maximum effectiveness. It is up to the coach to help his blockers find such a stance. This can be done by encouraging these techniques:

1. The heels of the feet should be raised off the ground slightly, putting weight slightly forward.
2. The coach can check weight distribution by looking at the blocker's profile and making certain that the tail is slightly higher than the head.

Balance

The next important part of the great stance is balance. Since balance is vital in the actual execution of the block, the coach should consider it equally as vital to the stance. For most players, balance is synonymous with "comfort." If the stance is comfortable it may also be balanced, but the coach should check the position of the feet for perfection of the stance. Line play is varied in what it entails, and many times a blocker will be hit from the side when he least expects it. It is therefore necessary for him to assume a wider stance than any other player. The proper width of the stance will vary with the player's weight, but generally it can be described as slightly wider than shoulder width. In the interest of comfort, many players will stagger one foot. The right-handed player will put his right hand down on the ground and drop his right foot back. The left-hander will do just the opposite. A proper gauge of this stagger distance would be heel-to-toe as a rule. (See Diagram 1-1.)

Right-Handed Blocker   Left-Handed Blocker

DIAGRAM 1-1

Visibility

When we refer to visibility in blocking, we are actually saying that you can't block what you can't see! The perfect stance should allow the blocker to see the defenders immediately in front of him, regardless of whether they are defensive linemen or linebackers.

The blocker must also be able to see defenders in either gap, for these are all the people that he would have to be responsible for blocking on a given play directed in his area. In order to insure this visibility, the blocker should not choose a stance that forces his head to look toward the ground. He must try to get as much height out of his stance as possible. This can be accomplished in part by using a two-point stance. This stance is used almost exclusively in the kicking game; however, it does not allow the blocker maximum quickness straight ahead. A four-point stance is also popular with coaches who emphasize straight ahead, one-on-one blocking, but here again a blocker is at a disadvantage when trying to pull out of the line. So much of his weight is distributed and spread out that pulling to trap or lead end-runs is difficult. The stance that we feel allows for maximum visibility, without denying the blocker the use of any of his techniques, is the three-point stance. Therefore, throughout this book, we will advocate the use of the three-point stance with all blocking types discussed. As a final extra technique which makes the stance even more conducive to the types of blocks in our system, we have the blockers put their fingertips on the ground instead of the knuckles. This gives them an extra bit of height and a more flexible surface from which they can push off on pulling assignments.

Power

The final element of the perfect block is power. Power is a form of potential energy in this case, for once the three-point stance has been perfected, the potential for power exists; otherwise, a successful, powerful block is just a case of luck. The complete description of the perfect three-point stance is as follows:

1. Feet slightly wider than shoulder width.
2. Toe of back foot even with heel of "up" foot.
3. Fingertips, not knuckles, on the ground.
4. Heels raised off the ground.
5. Tail end higher than head, with head up.

SPLITS IN THE LINE

The size of the split between linemen should be guided by the nature of each play. We believe in flexible rules for splits, and they are incorporated in each and every play. By doing this, the size of the split changes with the play and actually becomes part of our stance. This means that when we coach the proper stance, we are also demanding that the player know his split rules. In this way we not only get the blocker in the proper stance for each play, but we also have the exact split we want. The split changes in size as the play changes and is guided by the following rules:

1. If the play calls for a power block, such as a double-team, then the split between the two blockers will be tighter.
2. If the play calls for a cross block or an influence block, then the splits will be wider.
3. If the play is being run to the far side of any lineman, we have the lineman split wider to force the defender to split with him. This helps keep the defender farther away from the play.

4. If the play is being run to the same side of the lineman, then we ask him to tighten his split in order to keep the defender inside in a position where he can be hooked and prevented from pursuing to the outside.

The main point here is that when we stress the word "stance," we include the concept of splits between linemen with these guidelines in mind. The whole purpose of teaching proper line splits is to get the best angle on the defender in order to keep him far from the point of attack. Although many coaches may not employ this technique in the interior of their line, almost every coach uses a variation in the split of his receivers in order to alter defensive setups. A typical example is of course, the flex split used by the tight end when he is going to receive a pass as opposed to his tighter split when he is going to double-team with the tackle.

Throughout the course of the book, when we speak of proper stance, we also imply the technique of proper splits.

THE THREE COMMANDMENTS OF BLOCKING

All blocking is predicated on three basic commandments. In order they are:

1. *Quick start off the line of scrimmage.* The quicker off the ball a lineman is, the better are his chances of overcoming the defender's use of hands. Other defensive weapons such as slants, blitzes, forearm shivers and "reading" can be made ineffective by a quick charge.

2. *Good initial contact.* It is imperative that proper contact be made by the blocker to insure that he will be using the greatest surface area of his body to stop the defender's charge and ultimately move him out of the play. Depending on the defender's alignment and the block type being used, the surface of contact will vary from the blocker's shoulder to his hip.

3. *Acceleration on contact.* Once contact has been made, the blocker's next objective is to move the defender out of position. All too often the blocker concentrates his maximum efforts on quickness and initial contact, but falls to his knees because he did not accelerate his feet on contact. This is the most important aspect of all, for without it no block is truly a great one. Yet, if a blocker is too slow getting off the ball, or if he makes poor initial contact, he can still make a successful block by accelerating his feet when he does make contact. Many sports demand this technique also, only the word most commonly used to describe what we want here is "follow-through." In football, the term accelerate has more meaning since it demands that the blocker actually run faster.

There are many types of blocks that the offensive lineman can use to move a defender from any defensive alignment. In all situations the variables have nothing to do with the fundamentals of line play. The blocker must *always* have a perfect stance, he must *always* fire-out quickly off the ball, he must *always* make good initial contact, and he must *always* accelerate his feet on contact. The only adjustments may be the part of the body used to make contact with the defender or the steps taken to get to him, and these will be discussed in detail throughout the book. Adjusting the blocking surface is a technique that can be coached and, in many cases, used by the individual lineman at his own discretion.

THE DRIVE BLOCK

In this type of one-on-one block, the linemen use their eyes as an aiming device in order to keep sight of their target. The proper execution of the block is accomplished when the blocker slides his head to one side and drives his shoulder into the defender and, at the same time, brings his fists or forearms up into the defender's body. The actual blocking surface is the shoulder, fists or forearms and chest. The complete technique must be mastered and then put to use properly.

Techniques of the Drive Block

1. Start with a perfect stance.
2. Make good initial contact with the shoulder, forearms, and fists.
3. The block is complete when the blocker begins to accelerate and rises up to use his chest on the defender.

The drive block is used for blocking defenders in any position. The reasons for its use are many. First, let's suppose you are facing a defense that slants on the snap of the ball. The defender will line up in a head-on position, but, on the snap of the ball, he takes an angle step one way or another into the gap on one side of the blocker. If the blocker is quick off the ball and aims at his target with his eyes, making good initial contact, the slanting defender can be picked up on the blocker's shoulder. On the other hand, had the blocker aimed his shoulder at the defender as the surface of contact, the slanting technique would have caused him to miss the block entirely. It must be understood that contact is not to be made with the head, but this point of reference should serve as an aiming device in all our blocking.

1. Begin every drill with a perfect stance.

2. The proper initial step is taken and the head is up using the eyes as an aiming device.
3. Using the eyes as an aiming device enables the blocker to see the slanting action and get in front of the defender.
4. The block is complete when the blocker accelerates.

Rise-Up and Accelerate

As we begin to develop the techniques of the drive block, we add a technique called "rising up." We ask that our blockers try to arch their backs as they accelerate in an effort to stand up and run over the defender. This rising action makes the job of accelerating easier, and helps to get our blockers to carry out their blocks for a longer period of time. Furthermore, it enables the blocker to react to the tough defender who backs up and spins out. Rising-up can be drilled at half-speed against airshields and at full speed against a defender in a one-on-one situation. Since a certain amount of strength is required in order to execute this technique properly, we use the two-man sled or the seven-man sled to drill the rising-up action necessary in the drive block. The instructions below tell how this drill can be run.

Drilling for Rising-Up

1. The blockers take their stances directly in front of the sled pads and apply steady pressure to the machine. The coach encourages good body position in this phase.
2. On a command by the coach, the blockers must arch their backs and rise-up on the sled. They can immediately begin to accelerate their feet and drive the sled. On the coach's command they actually explode into the sled driving their fists or forearms into the pads.

THE NEAR SHOULDER BLOCK

This is perhaps the most common block used by offensive linemen. It is called near shoulder, because the blocker will use the shoulder *nearest* the defender to make initial contact. If the defender is on the blocker's left, he will make contact with the left shoulder, and vice versa. It is most effective when used against the defender who does not slant away from the blocker, but plays a more or less normal reading technique.

The near shoulder block is designed to move the defender down the line of scrimmage and away from the immediate point of attack. It is not very useful in preventing the defender from penetrating through the line of scrimmage. Practical uses for the near shoulder block would be:

1. Double-team blocking.
2. Trap blocking.
3. One-on-one blocking on dive plays.
4. Quick openers.

Very seldom is the defender in a head-on position. One reason is that this position gives neither the blocker nor the defender an advantage, unless of course the two linemen are mismatched in size and strength. Therefore, blockers are confronted with defenders who are in gaps to either side of them, stand-up defenders who play farther away from them, and even some defenders who play halfway on and halfway off one shoulder. (See Diagrams 1-2 through 1-5.)

Varying Defensive Alignments

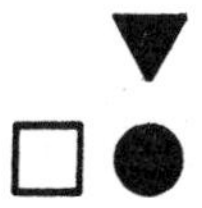

DIAGRAM 1-2: HEAD ON.

DIAGRAM 1-3: GAP.

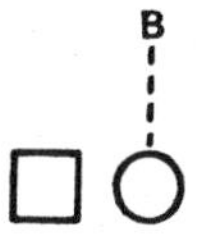

DIAGRAM 1-4: STAND-UP.

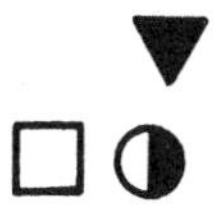

DIAGRAM 1-5: OUTSIDE SHOULDER.

The Step Drill

It therefore becomes vital that the initial step taken by the blocker gets him to the defender as quickly as possible through the shortest route. We teach our linemen to step directly toward the defender with the foot nearest the defender. Thus, if the defender we want to block is on our right side, we step with the right foot directly toward him on the initial step. That first step is vital to the entire block, for it puts the blocker in a good position to make a square, well-balanced block as quickly as possible. The blocker must remember this step technique for each and every block he uses, and we stress its importance with a simple axiom: "If you are to block to your right, then step to the right with your right foot, and if you are to block to your left, step to the left with your left foot." This simple but all-important technique is underemphasized by many coaches, and yet it should become a major part of your daily practice routine.

A very simple drill that we use called step drill can accomplish wonders in getting the blocker to make the correct initial step every time. A group of blockers are lined up in columns and rows facing their coach. From their proper stance, the blockers take one step in the direction specified by the coach's command. This drill also teaches unity in movement, and the coach can readily see which linemen are quicker than others. During the drill the coach must demand quickness and proper body balance. Since the step drill is a group drill, specific steps can be coached at the same time. For example, the step for a double-team block, or a trap block, or a cross block. Backfield steps can also be coached with this kind of a drill. While we are interested in only the initial step, we must emphasize quickness, balance and proper position. It is an excellent practice to teach the linemen to exaggerate that initial step even though in actual use it may only be a short jab step. By exaggerating its length, the execution becomes easier in a game situation. Therefore, putting all the basic fundamentals together, we have: a perfect stance, taking the initial step in the proper way and right direction, good initial contact with the proper surface of the body, acceleration of the feet on contact and, finally, rising-up on contact to take the defender past the point of attack.

THE FAR SHOULDER BLOCK

The techniques used in executing this type of shoulder block are basically the same as those described for the near shoulder block and are fundamentally the same techniques used in all forms of blocking. The front part of the chest, the forearms and the shoulder are the main contact surfaces used in the far shoulder block. An important note for the coach is that even though the far shoulder is being used as a blocking surface, the near foot is still the vital first step in getting to the defender. The major difference lies in the particular situation that calls for the use of this technique as opposed to other techniques. The far shoulder is defined as that shoulder farthest away from the defender to be blocked. A defender who is aligned to the blocker's right side would be attacked with the blocker's *left* shoulder; and conversely, if the defender were on the left side, he would be attacked with the blocker's *right* shoulder in a far shoulder block.

The far shoulder block derives its advantages from the fact that by its very nature it forces the blocker's body across and in front of the defender's route. This action, executed with some degree of force, prevents the defender from penetrating across the line of scrimmage and destroying the backfield action. For this reason it is not the kind of block that can be used to move defenders over a great distance, but rather to nullify their hard charge. Some practical applications of the far shoulder block are:

1. Blocking gap defenses.
2. Blocking for extra points and field goals.
3. Filling in for a pulling lineman.
4. Blocking down on the goal line, or in short yardage situations.
5. All plays such as sweeps, counters and reverses that take longer to develop than dives or quick openers.

In Diagrams 1-6 and 1-7, the blockers are using the "far" shoulder block to cutoff defensive penetration.

THE FAR SHOULDER BLOCK

1. Starting position showing the defenders in the gaps.

DIAGRAM 1-6

2. Note how their initial steps are in the direction of the defenders. The routes through the gaps are sealed off and penetration stopped. The shaded area indicates that each blocker is using a far shoulder block with the right shoulder.

DIAGRAM 1-7

CHAPTER 2

Combination Blocking

Combination blocking is a term that we use for describing the effective blocking of more than one lineman, executed at the point of attack. It is understood that while each man involved in the block is performing some variation of the one-on-one techniques described in Chapter 1, nevertheless, the success of the play is dependent upon the combined actions of all blockers involved. Combination blockers are used to add optional ways of blocking various defenses for the same play. In this way a team may gear itself for a set number of plays and run them with the utmost execution against all defenses by simply changing or redefining the blocking combinations to be used. As part of a regular set of running plays, combination blocks make possible such plays as the simple dive, the option, the veer, the sweep, the trap, the draw, the isolation and many other plays that add to a well-rounded offensive arsenal. In addition, there are times when combination blocks are necessary to overcome deficiencies, or to overcome some sort of disadvantage. A list of how combination blocks might serve your offensive system follows:

1. To add power at the point of attack as in a short yardage situation or on the goal line.
2. To get more blockers to the point of attack than there are defenders (as in the sweep or option).
3. To aid in adjusting the blocking to variations in defensive sets (as in the case of multiple-defense teams).
4. To help one blocker who may be weaker than his defensive opponent in a one-on-one situation.
5. To help overcome the power and skill of one or more particular defenders.

Regardless of how the combinations of blocks are used, the basic fundamentals are still the same as those for one-on-one techniques.

Every blocker must begin with the perfect three-point stance; every blocker must take the correct initial step; every blocker must fire-out quickly; every blocker must make good initial contact; and every blocker must rise-up and accelerate on contact. In this chapter we will describe some common types of combination blocks and also diagram them against various defensive sets.

THE DOUBLE-TEAM BLOCK

Double-team blocking is essential if power is to be a part of your offense. The double-team block assigns two blockers to move one defender. Its purpose is to create an opening at the point of attack that is too wide for a pursuing defender to fill alone. It also has the effect, if executed properly, of sealing off pursuit from the inside by linebackers. Some offensive formations lend themselves to the use of double-team blocking more than others; however, the following diagrams illustrate the most common uses of the double-team block with the formations and backfield actions that go with the specific play-types. (See Diagrams 2-1 through 2-4.)

One special characteristic of the double-team block is brought out by Diagrams 2-1 through 2-4: that any pair of linemen can execute this technique on any given play. The factor that decides which pair of blockers will use the block is the defensive setup. In several instances in the diagrams, the linebackers are left unblocked by direct assignment. The intention with these types of plays is to provide the ball carrier with maximum daylight at the immediate point of attack for such cases as short yardage or goal line efforts. In those situations, a linebacker's tackle three yards off the line of scrimmage is usually meaningless anyway. Furthermore, the proper execution of the double-team should make pursuit from the inside very difficult.

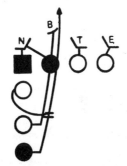

DIAGRAM 2-1: I FORMATION.
Isolation play with guard/center double-team.

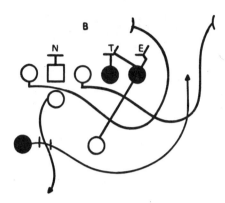

DIAGRAM 2-2: SPLIT-T FORMATION.

Sweep play with tackle/end double-team.

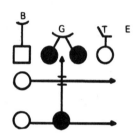

DIAGRAM 2-3: T FORMATION

Dive/Option series with guard/tackle double-team.

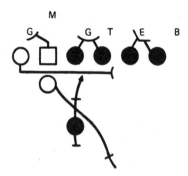

DIAGRAM 2-4: UNBALANCED FORMATION.

Draw-trap play with two powerful double-team blocks.

Terms Can Be Confusing

Although it is comfortable for us to speak in terms of double-team blocking, many coaches are more familiar with such terms as "two-on-one," "the shoot block," "the power block," "post-and-lead" and "post-and-drive" blocking. Our feeling about these different terms is that they have more meaning for the coach than they do for the players. As the diagrams will show, each of these techniques fits our definition of double-team blocking. The major difference in their names is due to the fact that they are used against different defensive positions. The confusion among players will arise when an opponent uses multiple defenses, and the blockers see several different sets for one particular play. This forces them to think, "Am I the post man or the drive man on this block?" "Do I use a power block or a shoot block against this defensive set?" The questions and the doubt go on to cause hesitation which destroys the block from the very first. Diagrams 2-5 through 2-8 will illustrate this point.

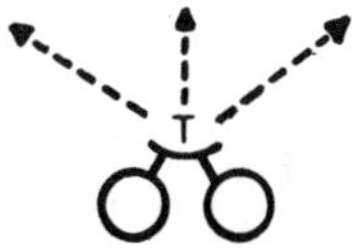

DIAGRAM 2-5: TWO-ON-ONE BLOCK.

This technique is executed on a defender aligned in the gap between blockers. The purpose of the block is simply to move the defender out of the point of attack in any direction possible.

Diagrams 2-6 through 2-8 show how an effective double-team block will seal-off the linebacker's pursuit and force him to loop around the blockers.

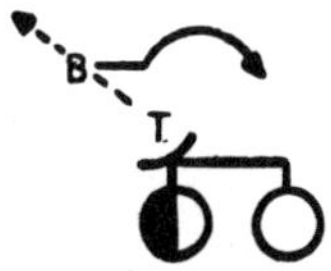

DIAGRAM 2-6: THE SHOOT BLOCK.

This technique is executed against the defender aligned on the inside shoulder of the inside blocker. The purpose of the block is to force the defender deep to the inside creating a large gap at the point of attack and sealing off inside pursuit from the linebacker.

DIAGRAM 2-7: THE POWER BLOCK.

This block-type is executed against the defender who is aligned head on the inside blocker. The inside blocker must set up the defender so that the outside blocker can come down on him and in unison turn the defender down the line of scrimmage to open the hole and seal off inside pursuit from the linebacker.

DIAGRAM 2-8: THE POST AND LEAD BLOCK.

This technique is executed against the defender who is aligned outside of the point of attack and must be taken inside. The outside blocker does the "setting up" in the *post* portion of the block, while the inside blocker must *lead* around to drive the defender to the inside.

By sticking to the basic terminology that states exactly what we want on every play, against every defense, the blockers are not concerned so much with direction, or specific technique. Regardless of the position of the defender, if a double-team block is called for, the two blockers involved will execute their assignments. To illustrate the difference between usage of terminology that changes with the defense and the consistency of using one term, the diagrams show blocking for one special play against two different defenses. In Diagrams 2-9 and 2-10, the blockers have to use entirely different techniques, while in Diagrams 2-11 and 2-12, the blockers execute the same double-team block on the same defender. The result shows that the defender goes a different way when blocked with the double-team.

With this simplification in terminology the blockers are concerned only with the technique of their block. The four considerations are as follows:

1. How is the initial step to be taken toward the defender?
2. What part of my body will I use for initial contact?
3. What must I do to prevent the defender from penetrating?
4. Which is the easiest possible direction for me to move the defender?

Fullback Off-Tackle Play

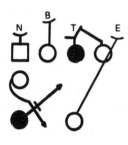

DIAGRAM 2-9

Power block vs. 5-2 defense.

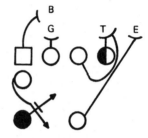

DIAGRAM 2-10

Post and lead block vs. 4-4.

Fullback Off-Tackle Play

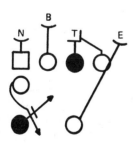

DIAGRAM 2-11

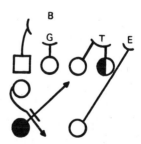

DIAGRAM 2-12

Five Steps to Double-Team Blocking

The techniques of double-team blocking can be described as an expanded form of two separate one-on-one blocks "combined" on the same defender. Both linemen must step directly toward the defender on their first step with the near foot. This step is the first vital technique that is so essential if the double-team block is to be soundly executed. It has the effect of getting the blockers to the defender quickly and also of closing the gap between them so that the defender will not be able to split them apart.

The second technique is learning which part of the body should be used in making initial contact. Both blockers should make contact with a drive block (see Chapter 1). We encourage this for the simple reason that circumstances may arise where one of the blockers does not get to his assignment. If this happens, for whatever reason, each blocker must be prepared to take the defender one-on-one, and this is our best way of handling the one-on-one situation.

The third technique can not be introduced unless both blockers are in contact with the defender. Assuming that both blockers have successfully executed the first two techniques, they must combine their efforts to complete the block. Since the two blockers have made contact, the seam or gap between them must be closed to prevent the defender from splitting them. The desired effect is to have two blockers moving as one unit. In order to accomplish this the blockers are taught to "feel" each other's presence and slide off their drive blocks and resort to a near shoulder block. The idea of feeling each other's presence is not an abstract thing, because the points of contact between the two blockers are the inside shoulders and hips. When these areas are properly connected, the gap between the blockers is closed. Daily drilling at very slow speeds to develop this feel for each other's presence is the only way the technique can be mastered. The coach should start the blockers off with a walk-through technique for many trials. Gradually, the tempo increases until the desired results are obtained in live scrimmage work.

The fourth technique teaches the blockers how to move the defender the easiest way possible. In actuality, as the blockers make contact with the defender they have a fairly good idea which way they will try to take him. The defender who plays head-on one of the blockers will probably slant one way or another, and this defender will simply be taken the way he wants to go, beyond the point of attack. Defenders who remain stationary will be driven in the direction of least resistance, while the defender who plays in the gap between the blockers will be driven straight back.

The fifth and final technique is the most important. Many years ago the double-team was successful if it simply buried the defender right where he was, but with today's sophisticated defensive techniques, such as spinning out, slanting, and reading, offensive blockers must follow through after contact and maintain their blocks until the play is whistled dead by the referee. In order to complete the follow-through in the double-team block, we drill our blockers daily on the technique of rising-up and accelerating. This drill does not add a new dimension to our daily routine because it is a desirable aspect of every type of block in our system. In summary then, the techniques of expert double-team blocking are:

1. Both blockers must take the correct initial step.
2. Both blockers attack the defender with a drive block anticipating that they will have to block him alone.
3. Both blockers "feel" for each other's shoulder and hip to close the gap between them.
4. Both blockers work as a single unit to move the defender in the easiest direction.
5. Both blockers must rise-up and accelerate as a means of following through.

THE CROSS BLOCK

In modern football, defenses have learned how to combat many one-on-one blocking patterns by showing the offense a variety of alignments. The relative success with which you are able to run your plays against these ever-changing alignments depends largely on how you are able to adjust your blocking patterns. One of the simplest ways to achieve this adjustment is to switch the blocking assignments between two linemen at the point of attack. In effect, the defense has probably shifted in such a way as to deprive blockers of an easy angle of approach for their block; therefore, switching the assignments between blockers should give the advantage back to the offensive linemen. The act of switching assignments between two blockers is called cross blocking and a clear example of its use and effectiveness can be seen in Diagrams 2-13 and 2-15.

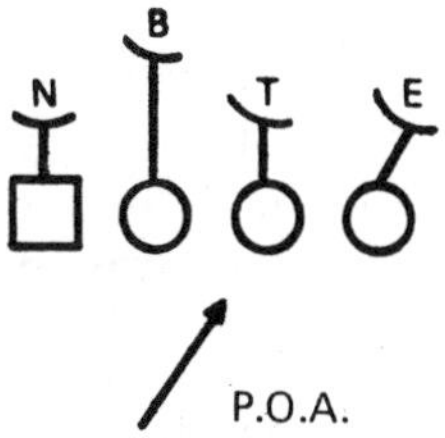

P.O.A.

DIAGRAM 2-13

Sound one-on-one blocking vs. 5-2 regular.

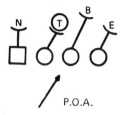

DIAGRAM 2-14

"Eagle" adjustment makes one-on-one blocking inadequate on defensive tackle.

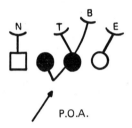

DIAGRAM 2-15

Cross block adjusts nicely for this play vs. "eagle" shift.

Note how the play being run in all situations is the same, yet the blocking patterns must change in order to adjust to the defensive shifts. If the blocking pattern does not change, as against the ""eagle" alignment, then the defensive tackle will not be blocked adequately. A simple switching of assignments as in the cross block makes the necessary adjustment.

Who Moves First? Fold

Since cross blocking involves two linemen, the problem of which man moves first arises. In order to distinguish the two different possibilities, we use two separate terms, the first of which is the "fold" technique. "Fold" describes that type of cross block where the outside lineman will step first toward the defender and the inside lineman will step around behind him. The relationship of outside and inside between linemen is explained as follows:

1. If the center and guard are to execute the fold technique, the guard is the outside lineman and moves first.

2. Between guard and tackle, the tackle is considered outside and he moves first.

3. Where the end and tackle are involved in the fold technique, the end will move first as he is outside the tackle.

Diagrams 2-16 through 2-18 clearly show the routes taken by the outside and the inside linemen in the three combinations just discussed for the fold technique.

The advantages of using the fold technique in these three examples should be obvious. First, in the center/guard point of attack, the center is able to execute a one-on-one block against a defender playing head-on, but because he must snap the ball before moving too far forward, he will have difficulty blocking a quick linebacker. Therefore, since the fold technique requires that he move second in the crossing action, it is more conducive to his blocking assignment. The main objective in crossing the blockers is to relieve them of the difficulty of a straight one-on-one situation where they might get beat by a bigger, stronger defender. The cross block gives each blocker the extra advantage of the angle approach as well as the "sneak attack."

Cross blocking has another side which will be discussed subsequently, but it's important to note that just as in the case of the one-on-one techniques and as in the case of the double-team block, all basic drills and training methods can be used to drill for the cross block. The coach should begin his earliest training as a walk-through drill and gradually work up to full-speed contact work. A second method of cross blocking is called "bingo" in our system.

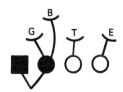

DIAGRAM 2-16: CENTER/GUARD FOLD.

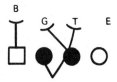

DIAGRAM 2-17: GUARD/TACKLE FOLD.

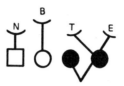

DIAGRAM 2-18: TACKLE/END FOLD.

Bingo

This technique, which we have come to call Bingo, is no more than the fold technique in reverse. In this crossing technique, the inside lineman will move first and the outside lineman will step around behind him. Diagrams 2-19 through 2-21 show how the combinations work against different defenses.

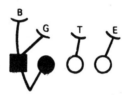

DIAGRAM 2-19: CENTER/GUARD BINGO.

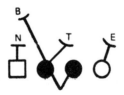

DIAGRAM 2-20: GUARD/TACKLE BINGO.

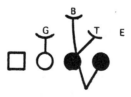

DIAGRAM 2-21: TACKLE/END BINGO.

To remind you, the following list of coaching points will aid in the teaching of these two techniques.

1. Regardless of whether the technique is fold or bingo, the first man to move must step in the proper direction with his near foot.

2. Each blocker should attack the defenders with a sound drive block.

3. The second blocker takes a jab step with his near foot to allow the first man to pass avoiding collision. There is no waiting or delay per se; this jab step is sufficient.

4. Upon contact, both blockers must rise-up and accelerate.

Once the timing of the steps is perfected, these variations of cross blocking can be used against all defenses in any offensive series. The best example of this statement is to mention the fullback veer play off the wishbone formation and triple option series. As most coaches know, many blocking assignments in the triple option consist of basic blocking with no pulling and little combination blocking. Defenses have risen to the occasion and reset their tackles, linebackers and ends into an eagle alignment to stop the fullback veer. In Diagrams 2-22 and 2-23, we see how basic blocking against the eagle alignment breaks down and how the use of a crossing technique, fold, nullifies the defense and improves the same play.

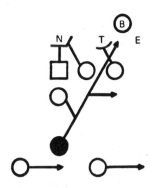

DIAGRAM 2-22

Basic blocking pattern for triple option series leaves linebacker unblocked in vital position.

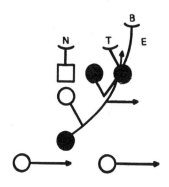

DIAGRAM 2-23

Guard/tackle fold technique nullifies advantages
of Eagle alignment.

What Determines the Usage of Fold as Opposed to Bingo?

There are several key factors that make this decision relatively easy
once they are understood.

1. The point of attack determines which pair of linemen are going
   to be involved in cross blocking. The linemen must know
   without a doubt which areas or holes are their responsibility.
   (See Diagram 2-24.)

DIAGRAM 2-24

2 hole = center/guard; 4 hole = guard/tackle;
and
6 hole = tackle/end.

2. The blocker who will move first is the blocker who is not
   covered head-on by a defensive lineman. The blocker who is
   covered head-on is the disadvantaged blocker, and he will jab
   step around behind his teammate. Fold or bingo are just terms
   that determine where the head-on defender is lined up. (See
   Diagrams 2-25 and 2-26.)

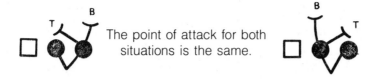

The point of attack for both situations is the same.

DIAGRAM 2-25: FOLD BLOCK.   DIAGRAM 2-26: BINGO BLOCK.

THE TRAP BLOCK

The trap block is named after the type of play rather than as a special blocking technique. The play is used to "sucker" a hard charging lineman to penetrate the line of scrimmage without blocking him with the blocker who is head-on him. The actual block comes from an offensive lineman who pulls from the opposite side of the line and makes contact from the blind side. By the time the defender realizes what is going to happen it is usually too late to do anything more than take on the blocker one-on-one. Therefore, once again, we are describing a special one-on-one technique of blocking.

Trap Sequences

Some typical trap plays have been diagrammed below showing how defenders in all positions may be "trapped," and how any one of several different offensive linemen can execute the trap technique. (See Diagrams 2-27 through 2-29.)

The trap as a play is only as good as the trap technique of blocking. There are many coaching points that must be understood before the trap can be run with its full effectiveness. The first coaching point is the manner in which the all-important first step is taken. As in every other block we have talked about thus far, and like each block we will discuss in future chapters, the blocker must take his initial step in the immediate direction of the defender's position with his near foot. In the case of a trap block, if the blocker is going to trap right, he must step initially to the right with his right foot. The procedure for trapping to the left is completely reversed. In addition to stepping in the right direction and with the proper foot, the trapper must step *into* the line of scrimmage, taking an inside route to the defender. The importance of this step can not be overlooked, for if the blocker fails to take an inside position on his first step, he will be completely out of position to trap the defensive player who waits or reads at the line of scrimmage. The trap block should be coached against three defensive charge routes, as follows:

1. The worst route the defender can take is *no* route at all. This is the "waiver."
2. The second most dangerous route is the one-step read which puts the defender right on the line of scrimmage.

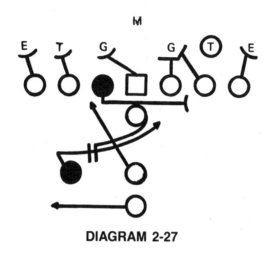

DIAGRAM 2-27

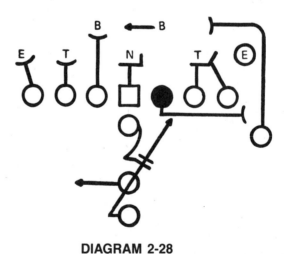

DIAGRAM 2-28

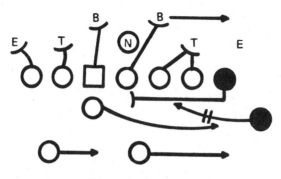

DIAGRAM 2-29

3. The third route is the best route for trap blocking. This is the over-penetration that goes deeper than the backfield.

The trapper must assume that the defender will take the worst possible route and compensate for this by stepping into the line of scrimmage to give himself the best angle shot at the defender. Diagrams 2-30 through 2-35 show how the blocker's route will hurt or help him in trapping the defender in the three possible situations.

Diagrams 2-30 through 2-32 illustrate that the lateral pulling route taken by the trapper is only effective against two of the three possible defensive charges. In Diagrams 2-33 through 2-35, note how the trapper takes an inside angle into the line and is always on target to block the defender regardless of the charge he makes.

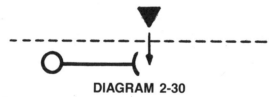

DIAGRAM 2-30

Defender reads but can still be trapped by blocker.

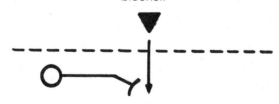

DIAGRAM 2-31

Defender over-penetrates and is easily trapped.

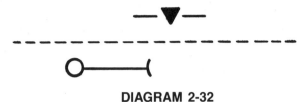

DIAGRAM 2-32

Defender waits or slants and can not be trapped with this angle.

DIAGRAM 2-33

DIAGRAM 2-34

DIAGRAM 2-35

The inside angle taken by the trapping lineman accommodates all types of defensive charges and slants.

Initial Contact Is Important

Contact is the next most important phase of the trap and there are several ways that contact can be made with success. The first and foremost technique is, of course, the drive block. Since the blocker and defender are relatively far away from each other, there is the distinct possibility that the defender could react and avoid the trap block by backing up or moving out of the way. By using the drive block, the trapping lineman is assuring himself maximum visibility and maximum contact area. Should the defender try to slip away from the contact, the blocker can always slide off into a shoulder block and accelerate still with a good surface area for driving.

The second way that the trap block may be executed is with the near shoulder block. The problem with shoulder blocking on the trap is that the blocker may use the wrong shoulder. When trapping to the right, if the blocker were to use his left shoulder, the defender could easily slip to the inside and destroy the play. Therefore, when coaching the use of a shoulder block for trapping, this simple rule must be memorized: "In order to TRAP to the right, step first with the right foot and block with the right shoulder"; "TRAP left...step left...left shoulder."

A FINAL WORD ABOUT PRECISION

At this point we should emphasize the need for precision in the execution of combination blocks. Whether the block involves a double-team, a cross, a short trap or a long sweep, since the techniques have become more complicated, the time spent perfecting these techniques should increase proportionally. The reasoning is basic: If more than one blocker is executing more than one technique, all of which are vital to the success of one particular play, the chances for error have increased greatly and the success of the play is in jeopardy without precision developed through adequate practice time. Therefore, we do not recommend that your entire offensive system and play-types be decided by combination blocking, but that whichever plays do require these combined techniques receive sufficient practice and drill time.

CHAPTER **3**

Individual Blocking Techniques

The old proverb, "Football is a game of blocking and tackling," is very true, but neither blocking nor tackling alone makes up good football. A lineman who can block well because he is bigger and stronger than his opponent will eventually lose his advantage to a defender who is quicker and plays his position with finesse and technique. In modern football, defensive stars are not flat-footed in their stance, waiting to challenge a blocker in a man-on-man battle. Stunts, slants and loops are the order of the day, and if the offensive linemen are to keep pace with the defenders' tactics, they too must develop blocking techniques and finesse. Realizing that football has become a game of techniques, we have adopted several blocking techniques that make blocking successful against the modern defensive weapons. We advocate the use of these techniques as a means for sophisticating the individual line play of your centers, guards, tackles and tight ends. Furthermore, it is hoped that once mastered, these techniques will be employed by your linemen at their own discretion. In this way, the defender is not only in doubt as to the point of attack, or the starting count, or who will block him, but also *how he will be blocked.* The essential ingredients of full acceptance of these techniques are open-mindedness and common sense.

THE CARTWHEEL BLOCK

Defenders who play head-on a blocker are the most difficult people to block. This is true for several reasons:

1. If the defender is bigger and stronger than the blocker, we have a one-on-one mismatch.

2. Defenders who are head-on usually are in this position to execute some sort of stunt or slant.

3. The inexperienced offensive lineman tends to wait or hesitate, allowing the defender to beat him on the initial charge.

28

4. Since the defender is allowed to use his hands, the blocker's head and shoulders are prime targets for a quick shot at the snap of the ball.

The blocker most troubled by this situation is the offensive center, for unlike the other blockers, he must snap the football at the same time he fires-out to make contact. Another disadvantage that the center endures, is that most of the time the defender playing head-on him is very close to his nose. Unlike the guard's man or the tackle's man who are slightly off the ball, the center must be prepared to take a defensive shot immediately, and because of these factors many centers get beat by a good nose-guard's quick charge. Although the technique of cartwheel blocking can be used by any blocker who is faced with a head-on defender, we offer it as an individual technique for centers against the 5-man defense and the nose-guard.

The purpose of the cartwheel block is to nullify the defender's charge, avoid contact with the defender's hands and arms, and prevent the defender from pursuing the play. By no means, however, will this block move a defender very far or "blow" him out of the hole. If executed properly, the cartwheel block will eliminate the defender from the play entirely.

Execution of the cartwheel block is similar to the scramble block as far as contact and initial movement are concerned. The blocker must get his shoulders and helmet under the defender's groin area in a lunge or explosion off the line of scrimmage. At the instant contact is made the actual cartwheel action comes into use. The blocker whips his hips to the right or left, depending on which way the play is going, and makes a complete 180-degree turn on all fours. If the play goes to the right, then he whips his hips to the right, and conversely for a play that goes to the left. The term "cartwheel" emphasizes the necessity for the whipping action of the hips in order to bring the blocker around 180 degrees. This position prevents the defender from pursuing laterally to the point of attack. Diagrams 3-1 through 3-4 depict the steps in execution of the cartwheel technique.

Some coaching points should be stressed here if the cartwheel block is to be perfected:

1. Make initial contact with a scramble block.

2. Accelerate before turning the hips to cartwheel.

3. Whip the hips to the side of the point of attack until you are 180 degrees from where you started.

In the event that you notice the defender getting away from this block, there are two points that should be checked. First, it is possible that the blocker is too conscious of turning his hips and is not making proper initial contact first. He must scramble block his opponent first, *then,* cartwheel. The second thing to watch is whether or not the blocker is truly whipping his hips around the defender. The cartwheel technique should be so quick that the blocker actually leaves his feet in the process of whipping. He should not mistake this action for a crab-type walk.

The main idea of blocks and techniques like these is to teach your offensive lineman that brain can defeat brawn. No physical requirements are necessary for the cartwheel block, yet it is a valuable weapon to be used against the defender who lines up head-on and tries to outmuscle the blocker.

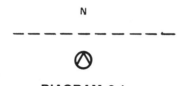

DIAGRAM 3-1

The center vs. nose-guard.

DIAGRAM 3-2

Initial contact made with scramble technique.

DIAGRAM 3-3

The blocker now begins to whip or cartwheel his hips.

DIAGRAM 3-4

The completed block shows the head and feet are 180 degrees from the original starting point and the defender is cut off from pursuit.

THE CHECK BLOCK

The check block is little more than a far shoulder block used on a *specific play* by a *specific lineman* with a *specific purpose.* The play type that requires the use of the check block is any play where one or more interior linemen pull out of the line to trap a defender or help lead plays that go around the end.

The specific lineman involved in check blocking is any lineman playing directly next to the pulling blocker on the side nearest the point of attack. Diagrams 3-5 through 3-7 show several play types where one or more linemen are required to pull out, and the shaded figure indicates that lineman who would be using the check block.

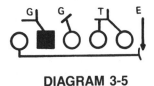

DIAGRAM 3-5

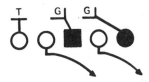

DIAGRAM 3-6

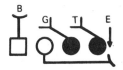

DIAGRAM 3-7

As the diagrams indicate, the check blocker is using this technique to prevent two things; first, to stop the penetration of the defender into the offensive backfield; and second, to stop the defender from pursuing the play laterally. These two purposes are not only specific, but also vital if the pulling lineman's block is to be effective.

Since the check block is nothing more than a far shoulder block, one might ask why the separate term? The reason is justified by the nature of the plays that require check blocking. For example, if we want our center to block any defender playing head-up on a pulling guard, we want him to stop the defender's penetration and pursuit. Having been coached several different ways to block a man one-on-one, the center may try to use a drive block or a scramble block or even a near shoulder block to carry out his assignment. However, these types of blocks are not sufficient to achieve our two purposes. Therefore, instead of asking the blocker to remember that he must use the far shoulder technique, we encourage him to think of his assignment as a check block. Having been given this term for the act of blocking for a pulling lineman, everyone is aware that only the far shoulder block will suffice. In the course of instructing the line in their blocking rules, we just include the term check block to mean the type of block used exclusively to block for a pulling lineman.

To reiterate the differences between the far shoulder block and the check block, we would say that the use of the far shoulder block is an option open to any blocker who feels that he can accomplish his assignment with it. But the check block is a precise block, mandatory in plays where one lineman must block the defender head-on a pulling lineman. The diagrams show how the check block serves all offensive lineman in different situations. (See Diagrams 3-8 through 3-10.)

A final technique that could add to the benefits of the check block would be the use of a cartwheel after contact. This would insure that the defender did not back off the line of scrimmage and avoid the check block. Since all the techniques of one-on-one blocking tend to overlap a great deal, the line coach should encourage the use of such techniques as an added part of each lineman's weapons system.

DIAGRAM 3-8

The left guard will pull out of line while the center must check the defender's penetration and pursuit.

DIAGRAM 3-9

Note how the first steps of the center and the guard seem to mesh, allowing both blockers to get their assignments as quickly as possible.

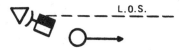

DIAGRAM 3-10

The guard is completely out of the line now, and the center has stopped the defender's penetration. Note how the check blocker is using the far shoulder block. (Shaded area).

THE SWEEP BLOCK—PRO STYLE

The sweep, or end-run as it is more commonly known, is as old as football itself. The theory of the sweep is to attack the flank of the defense with more blockers than the defense can handle. Outnumbering the defenders is of prime importance to the success of the sweep, and this can be accomplished by pulling one or more of the interior linemen and having them lead the ball carrier around the end. The best executors of the sweep are the professional athletes and coaches who have the natural talent to intensify the devastating effect of this powerful play. Our contention is, however, that the techniques involved

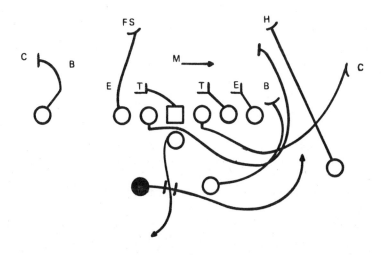

DIAGRAM 3-11
Pro sweep vs. 6-1 Defense.

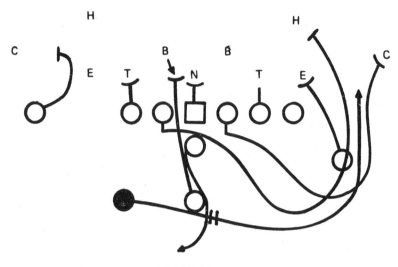

DIAGRAM 3-12

Right tackle and right end blocking scheme.

in running the sweep properly are wrapped-up almost entirely in the way the offensive linemen pull to lead the ball-carrier around the end. These techniques are taught in every pro football camp and can be adapted to the high school program if the coach's philosophy entertains the value of the sweep as an offensive weapon. We will further state, that no coach should waste the time of his staff or players by running any other facsimile of a sweep unless these special techniques are employed. The following diagrams illustrate several different offensive sets and how a sweep may be run from them (See Diagrams 3-11 and 3-12.)

Before we explain the blocking techniques, it is essential that an explanation of how the defense will react to a sweep or any end-run be given. A schematic explanation is given below.

The pursuit of the interior defensive linemen must be cut off by the blocking of the onside offensive end and tackle and possibly the wingback in some formations. But the rotating secondary are the defenders who must be blocked by the pulling linemen. For our purposes, we will talk in terms of the guards as being the pulling linemen, although many teams run the sweep successfully by pulling a guard and a tackle. Regardless of which linemen get the assignment, the techniques and responsibilities are the same.

The most immediate problem is the defender who first appears on the outside of the end. This will be the defensive cornerback in a 4-spoke defense, and the outside end in a 3-spoke defense. This defender is supposed to come up and meet the play from the outside in. The lead blocker is responsible for taking this defender one-on-one and hope-fully, kicking him *out*.

The second dangerous defender will be coming from the inside. He will be either the middle linebacker or the middle safety, depending on the assignment given to the wing or flanker-back. This defender is the responsibility of the trailing blocker and must be kept inside.

The defensive lineman must pursue the play laterally, down the line of scrimmage. (Diagram 3-13.)

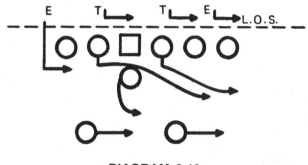

DIAGRAM 3-13

The defensive secondary must rotate toward the play from the outside-in, in order to prevent the ball carrier from getting outside the last defender. (Diagram 3-14.)

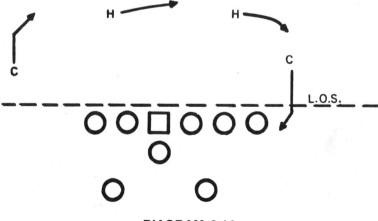

DIAGRAM 3-14

The inside linebackers must pursue the play at regular depth, laterally down the line of scrimmage. (Diagram 3-15.)

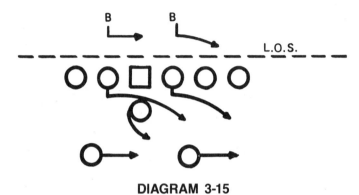

DIAGRAM 3-15

Diagrams 3-16 and 3-17 show the blocking scheme for the onside linemen and the lead blocker vs. two very common defenses. In Diagrams 3-18 and 3-19, the blocking schemes are designed against what is considered by most to be the pro defense and is most likely the best defense against the sweep. If you can block the pro defense effectively for the sweep, you should be able to block almost any other defensive set.

The pulling lineman face several problems on sweep plays, all of which involve timing of some sort:

1. If they get to the point of attack too soon, their defender will have time to recover from the block and still get in on the tackle.

2. If they do not meet the defender squarely, and face-to-face, they may lose their balance and execute a sloppy block or lose the defender altogether.

3. If one of the pulling linemen gets to the point of attack before the other, the running back will be forced to commit himself to a direction too soon. Furthermore, the idea of outnumbering the defenders will have been defeated.

It is obvious from these coaching points that the proper execution of the sweep as a play in general, demands discipline and constant practice. The blockers' techniques are discussed below.

The lead blocker's first step must be with the near foot in the direction of the sweep, but back on an angle of 45 degrees with the line of scrimmage. (See Diagram 3-20.)

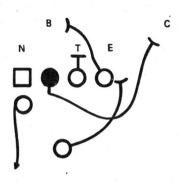

DIAGRAM 3-16

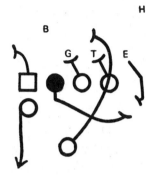

DIAGRAM 3-17

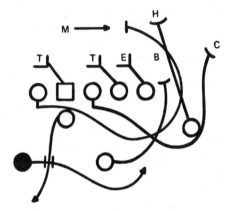

DIAGRAM 3-18

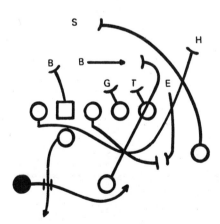

DIAGRAM 3-19

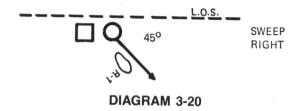

DIAGRAM 3-20

His second step is what we call a "leveling-off" step that gets his entire body on this 45-degree angle path with the line of scrimmage. (See Diagram 3-21.)

DIAGRAM 3-21

The third step begins to round off his route to eventually bring his body square with the line of scrimmage heading upfield toward the goal line. (See Diagram 3-22.)

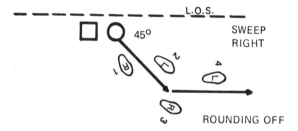

DIAGRAM 3-22

This series of steps represents an actual "loss" of about four yards. We refer to this as "getting depth," and it serves several purposes:

1. It enables the back to catch up with the blocker so that they are together when the block is actually made.

2. It puts the blocker in a better position to see how the defense is rotating and to find his blocking assignment.

3. It enables the blocker to face his opponent squarely and make an effective run-through block.

This looping technique is a method that should also be taught to the ball carrier for the same reasons. Diagrams 3-23, 3-24, and 3-25 show how all these steps put the lead blocker, defenders and ball carrier in the right position at the right time.

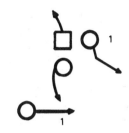

DIAGRAM 3-23

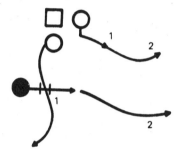

DIAGRAM 3-24

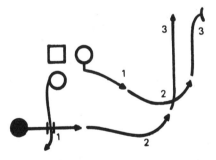

DIAGRAM 3-25

The trailing blocker's techniques are exactly the same, except for two points. The first point is that his initial two steps must be lateral so that he may clear the center's tail to allow the quarterback to make his pivot without colliding with him. This point differs from the initial steps taken by the lead blocker in that he will step off immediately on a

45-degree angle. On the trailing blocker's third step, which will be with his near foot, he will begin the 45-degree angle route taken by the lead blocker. From that point on he follows the same steps as the lead blocker until he gets to the line of scrimmage. The diagram helps clarify the actual steps taken by the trailing blocker. (See Diagram 3-26.)

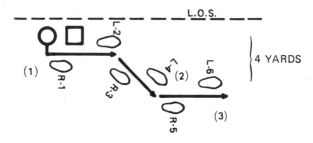

DIAGRAM 3-26

1. The number (1) shows the first step taken with the right foot to get the blocker out of the line. The second step taken with the left foot gets the blocker past the center's tail and allows the QB to pivot without collision.
2. The number (2) shows the steps taken in order to get depth required for timing. These are the same steps as those taken by the lead blocker.
3. The number (3) represents the "leveling-off" steps taken by the blocker so that he may approach the line of scrimmage with body and shoulders square.

As he approaches the line of scrimmage, the trailing blocker should be almost side-by-side with the lead blocker and to his inside. (See Diagram 3-27.)

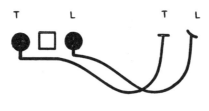

DIAGRAM 3-27

The trailing blocker must be conscious of pursuit from the inside, so as soon as he is facing up-field toward the goal line he must use his eyes and find the first enemy jersey to come from the inside. A technique we have used successfully to make certain that the trail blocker looks inside is to have him put his inside hand down on the ground and turn or pivot on it to the inside. Since the entire sweep play demands precision and discipline, it is one time we do not simply block the "first enemy jersey seen." Each man has a precise assignment and must carry out his technique until it can no longer be executed. For example, we do not tell the blockers *whom* to block, but we insist that they are in a definite position *where* they are to block. Namely, the lead blocker looks to the *outside* once he clears the end. Furthermore, both blockers must use the sweep technique in order to get where we want them. Unless these techniques and disciplines are perfected the sweep will not be successful, and by "successful," we mean it must average at least four yards per carry.

THE HOOK BLOCK

The final type of individual technique is one that allows the tight end to block the defensive end on wide plays such as options and quick pitches. As a technique, however, we think that all linemen should learn the proper execution of the hook block in the event that they may decide to use it in a given situation.

The hook block is so named because its objective is to prevent a defender who is already lined up on the blocker's outside to pursue to the outside. The blocker is attempting to take a defender who is aligned to his outside, to the inside. Normally, we do not ask our blockers to take a defender in any particular direction, but rather to take the defender in the direction he wants to go. But as you will see in the few play types that are diagrammed, hook blocking techniques can aid in the execution of some very quick and devastating plays. (See Diagrams 3-28 and 3-29.)

The basic problem in situations where the hook block is desirable is position. The blocker is in a very bad position to be taking the defender *in.* Therefore, the blocker's initial step will again be vital. He must step perfectly laterally on a parallel with the line of scrimmage, toward the defender. Some blockers may even find it beneficial to step back on the same 45-degree angle route that the pulling linemen used for the sweep block. The important thing is not to step directly at the defender, for in all probability he will be charging across the line of scrimmage, even if only one step, and this will destroy any chance the

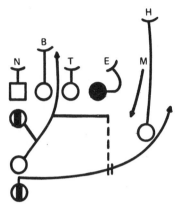

DIAGRAM 3-28

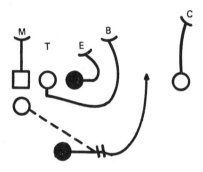

DIAGRAM 3-29

blocker has of hooking him. By taking this initial step, the blocker is giving himself better position on the defender and is also forcing the defender to make a choice as to where to charge. By stepping out or even back, the blocker has opened an alley to the inside that many defensive players will take. Therefore, we see that this position step has a two-fold purpose:

1. It puts the blocker in a better position to hook the defender to the inside.
2. It influences the defender to charge to the inside.

Once the advantage of position has switched to the blocker, he has a choice of two types of one-on-one to use. Keeping in mind that his assignment requires only that he keep the defender from pursuing to the outside, he can use the far shoulder block or the cartwheel block.

If the far shoulder block is used, the description of the entire blocking pattern for a blocker whose defensive counterpart was on his right would be as follows:

1. Step back or laterally with your right foot first, giving the defender an inside route to influence him to the inside.

2. Your next step should take you on a route toward the defender's outside hip. Your aiming device is your eyes.

3. Make contact with your *left* shoulder, forearm and side of helmet, acclerate and rise-up to turn the defender.

THE INFLUENCE BLOCK FOR TRAP PLAYS

We mentioned the word "influence" in the preceding section in the discussion of the hook block. The term is descriptive of the way offensive linemen can overcome the reading technique of defensive linemen. These reading tactics are also making it more and more difficult for teams to run trap plays or sweep plays with high degrees of success. The reading defender keys the blocker's moves and follows a set of rules that enable him to react to the proper pursuit angle without ever having to see the backfield action. Defenders who perform their reading skills well are extremely troublesome to offensive blocking that is anything other than straight one-on-one. The pulling lineman is an accurate key that will lead the defender to the play nine times out of ten since linemen are not often used for faking, as backs are.

Offensive blocking must sophisticate itself enough to compensate for the reading technique and once again take the advantage. By influencing the defender to do one thing, we can execute our blocking assignment more easily, and if the influence is good enough, the defender may in fact block himself. An example of how a reading defense can destroy the standard trap play is diagrammed below. (See Diagram 3-30.)

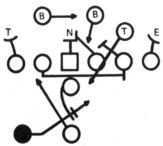

DIAGRAM 3-30

The reading in the diagram can be explained as follows:

1. Both linebackers will key the guards in front of them. When a guard double-teams, the linebacker fills quickly; when a guard pulls, the linebacker pursues laterally and finds the ball.

2. The defensive tackle being trapped jams into the inside because he reads the offensive tackle in front of him going inside.

The result is that the onside tackle is forced to block a linebacker who is coming hard; the trapping guard must block a defender who is bearing down on him, shortening the distance between them; and finally, a linebacker is in pursuit and free to make the tackle at the point of attack.

Many coaches feel that the best way to counteract the difficulty is to do trapping with a different lineman, namely, the offensive tackle, as shown in the diagram. But here again, the effects of reading are not being countered. (See Diagram 3-31.)

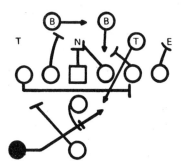

DIAGRAM 3-31

In order to force the defense to use its reading techniques against itself, we teach the influence technique to the onside tackle. Since we are trapping the defender playing in front of him, we want our offensive tackle to force the defender to read incorrectly. We feel that this influence technique will benefit our play more than the double-team block most coaches use along with the trap itself, as in the case of the onside guard and center double-teaming the nose-guard. Our blockers sacrifice the double-team block and rely on well-executed one-on-one techniques to make the trap go.

Influencing can be done in several ways, the first way is a "brush-and-slide" type of influence. The blocker doing the influencing, usually the offensive tackle, will make a very slight contact with the defender we want to trap. In other words, he will "brush" him. The influence blocker then slides off the tackle *to the outside* and blocks the first defender to show. It is imperative that the influence blocker slide to the outside, for if the tackle is reading properly, he will slide out with our influence man. (See Diagrams 3-32 and 3-33.)

Another way we can influence the defender is by faking pass protection. The influence blocker will set up in pass protection style and may even yell, "pass, pass..." to make the defensive lineman think that a pass is in the making. Any good defensive lineman knows that on passes he must rush the quarterback, and this little bit of faking often causes the defender to actually straighten-up and over-charge through the line of scrimmage. This makes trapping ever so easy. This form of influence blocking, however, is also accompanied by a brush-and-slide technique, so that instead of going directly at the defender, the influence blocker now drops back and influences the defender to over-penetrate, and then he slides out and picks up his assignment. (See Diagram 3-34).

Brush-Style Influencing with Either Type of Trap

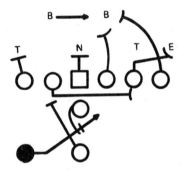

DIAGRAM 3-32: Guard Trap vs. 5-2.

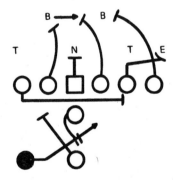

DIAGRAM 3-33: Tackle Trap vs. 5-2.

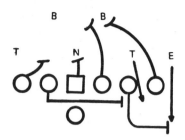

DIAGRAM 3-34

The right tackle fakes pass protection blocking and draws the defender in.

Finesse is the difference between those linemen who are good blockers and those who are great ones. The individual lineman who takes pride in his position should also have enough pride to practice and develop these techniques. We contend that these techniques will make the individual a more consistent blocker and a more confident part of your offensive line.

CHAPTER 4

Simple and Consistent Rule Blocking

Having been introduced to the many variations a defensive team can come up with, the coach must next ask, "How can my linemen block these variations with any degree of consistency?" This question can be answered in many different ways, and throughout this chapter we will offer you what we consider to be the best possible way to block multiple defenses. This is not to say, however, that other ways of blocking are not both simple and consistent. Our system was developed with several things in mind, and it is because of these considerations that we find our system to be simple and consistent. The main considerations are:

1. Rules eliminate the need for combination blocks. Therefore, coaching time is reduced.
2. No opponent is restricted to one alignment per game; expect a change on every play.
3. Never expect the defender to wait; anticipate movement from every defender and beat him off the line.

Finally, we treat our rules as priorities, meaning that if the blocker considers one rule first and it does not apply to the situation, then he will rely on his second rule or priority, and so on. As the chapter progresses, you will see how we accommodate such defensive variations as stacks, slants and other stunts. But, as in any introduction, we must learn terminology...

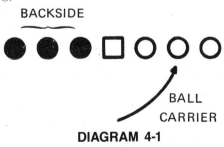

DIAGRAM 4-1

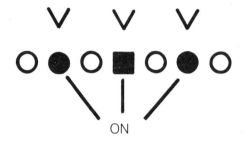

DIAGRAM 4-2

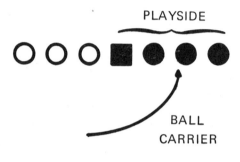

DIAGRAM 4-3

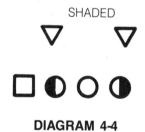

DIAGRAM 4-4

TERMINOLOGY

In order for your linemen to understand what you expect of them, you must develop a common language. Coaches today are very conscious of ways of expressing football terms so that they can be understood by their players and by other coaches. The following terms should be learned by all offensive linemen before they attempt to learn their blocking rules.

Backside: Refers to that part of the line of scrimmage farthest away from the point of attack. We also refer to offensive linemen who are beyond the center and away from the point of attack as, "backside linemen."

Example: If the play goes to any point on the right of center, the left guard, left tackle and left end are all "backside." (See Diagram 4-1.)

Gap: Refers to the area between offensive blockers. Thus, the area between guard and tackle split is the guard/tackle gap, and the area between the tackle-end split is the tackle/end gap, and so on.

On: Refers to that defender who plays directly in front of the blocker. (See Diagram 4-2.)

Over: Refers to that defender who plays directly in front of the blocker, but off the line of scrimmage. In all cases, this term refers to a linebacker.

Playside: The opposite of backside. That side of the offensive line closest to where the ball is being run. This includes the center, guard, tackle, and tight end when used as "playside" linemen.

Example: If a play is designed to go to the right, then the center, right guard, right tackle, and right end are all considered playside linemen. (See Diagram 4-3).

Point of Attack (P.O.A.): Refers to the exact area where the ball carrier is assigned to run. Many teams refer to the point of attack as the hole.

Shaded: This term refers to the position of the defender that puts him on the blocker's inside or outside shoulder. (See Diagram 4-4.)

Slant: Refers to a defensive maneuver whereby two things may happen:

1. A defender who is "on" will slant to a gap.
2. A defender who is aligned in a gap will slant to a position "on" a blocker. (See Diagrams 4-5, 4-6.)

Example 1.

DIAGRAM 4-5

Example 2.

DIAGRAM 4-6

Special Plays: Refers to any play where one or more linemen are required to pull out of their normal position. Specific play types would be traps, powers and sweeps.

Stack: Name given to a defensive alignment where two defenders occupy the same area, one directly behind the other. The stack may occur in the on position or the gap position. (See Diagram 4-7, 4-8.)

Straight Plays: Refers to any play other than those that are "special." No lineman will pull out of the line and all blocking will be basically "straight."

Inside: The term applies to the position of the center of our offensive line. If we say "inside gap," the implications are different for each lineman. Diagram 4-9 shows the blocking pattern as it would look if the linemen were to block their "inside gap."

BLOCKING RULES FOR STRAIGHT PLAYS

As the definition above states, straight plays are those which require only straight-ahead blocking. Specific play-types would be dives, slants, sneaks, and options. In none of these plays do we attempt to block the defenders at the ends or corners. Any play that we want to attack these areas uses special blocking, e.g., pulling linemen. Therefore, with this in mind we can set up our blocking patterns without concerning ourselves with the wide defenders. Our rules for these straight plays are as follows:

1. Block the defender in the playside gap.
2. If no defender is in the playside gap, then block the defender playing in the on position.
3. If no defender is in the on position, block the defender in the over position.
4. If no defender is playside gap, on, over, then block backside areas.

As you will quickly see, these rules are presented in terms of priorities. They attempt to cover every possible alignment the defense can assume near the blocker. Naturally, we do not require that our linemen learn these rules in such a long, and verbose style; we abbreviate the rules to read as follows: "For any straight play, block playside gap, man on, over, or backside." It is imperative that each blocker think in that order.

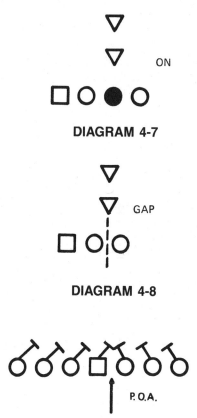

DIAGRAM 4-7

DIAGRAM 4-8

DIAGRAM 4-9

Practical Applications

In the subsequent diagrams we will show how these simple rules can accommodate a multitude of defensive alignments for the same play and thereby demonstrate the consistency of this rule system. For the sake of the diagrams, we will use the following hole numbering system as a source of reference. These hole are, in effect, our points of attack, and we demand that every linemen know the location of every point of

attack relevant to his own position. This goes along with the require-
ment that every lineman know the terminology perfectly. (See Diagram
4-10).

The first play (Diagram 4-11) will be a simple dive play through the
1 hole against several defensive sets. Remember that the rules are:
playside gap, on, over, and then backside.

Now let's take the same basic play and run it against an odd
defensive alignment. Note how our priorities accommodate this defense. (See Diagram 4-12.)

Now that we have diagrammed an offensive line with hole numbers, the word "playside" has significant meaning, for now the linemen
who are nearest the point of attack know exactly where the ball is being
run. The advantage of this type of numbering and priority blocking has
a tremendous value in goal line situations, for there is no need for a
special set of goal line blocking rules. In the diagrams that follow,
several points may be attacked with powerful blocking that more than
accommodates the gap 8 defense, a defense used very often in short
yardage and goal line situations. (See Diagrams 4-13, 4-14.)

These few examples show how consistent the rules can be for open
field defenses and short yardage defenses. Now we will take a look at the
more sophisticated stacked defenses.

Rule Blocking vs. Stacked Defenses

Stacked defenses pose the greatest problem for a team's blocking
rules simply because most rules depend on the alignment of the
defenders before the ball is put into play. In reality, the stack alignment
does its work after the ball is snapped, and unless the blockers know
what to expect from the stack in front of them, confusion sets in.
Stacked defenses do not pose a great problem for our rules because we
take the time to teach the theoretical use of stacks, and we block
according to those possibilities. Diagram 4-15 shows two different ways
that an on stack can stunt against the offense.

DIAGRAM 4-10

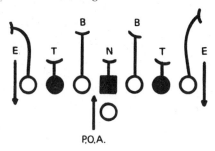

P.O.A.

DIAGRAM 4-11: Dive Through the 1 Hole vs. 5-2 Regular.

1. Both ends have resorted to their last priority: backside.
2. Both tackles are blocking according to their second rule: on.
3. Both guards block their third priority: over.
4. The center blocks the man on.

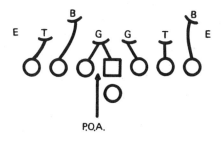

P.O.A.

DIAGRAM 4-12

1. Left guard and center block according to their first priority: playside gap.
2. Left tackle and left end also block playside.
3. Right tackle blocks man on, his second priority.
4. Right end has no man on, so he blocks third priority which is man over.

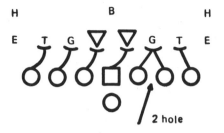

DIAGRAM 4-13: A 2-Hole Play vs. the Gap 8.

1. Each man is blocking playside gap, #1 priority.
2. We get an automatic double-team block at the 2 hole.

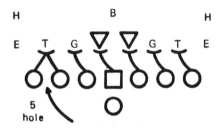

DIAGRAM 4-14: A 5-Hole Play vs. the Gap 8.

1. Each man is blocking according to his first priority, playside.
2. Again, we get an automatic double-team block at the 5 hole.

DIAGRAM 4-15: The Stacked Defense On Position.

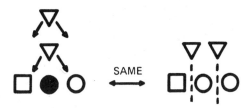

DIAGRAM 4-16

We consider the on stack to be the same as a gap defense.

When the stack is on as in Diagram 4-15, the offensive lineman must assume that some sort of stunt is in the making. Very seldom will a stacked alignment remain stationary after the ball is put into play. By virtue of the on position, we contend that the only effective slant will be when the defenders attack the gaps on either side of the blocker. It is possible for them to slant over to the center's nose or over to the tackle's nose, but I doubt that this distance could be covered effectively. Thus, any blocker who sees a stack on him, automatically assumes that on the snap of the ball at least one of the defenders will be in his inside gap and one will be in his outside gap. The right tackle is also aware of the possible outcome of the stack that is on his guard. He anticipates that on the snap of the ball there will be a defender in his inside gap. And finally, the center, too, is aware of the stack on the guard. He assumes that on the snap of the ball one of the defenders will be in the gap between himself and the right guard. In effect, the gap setup we have diagrammed is blocked or attacked with our priorities the same way as a gap defense would be. (See Diagram 4-16.)

The next diagram shows the blocking pattern in accordance with our rules for the on stack as compared to the gap defense. (See Diagram 4-17.)

A second way that a stacked alignment may be used against the offense is in the gap between two blockers. Several common gap stacks appear in Diagrams 4-18, 4-19, 4-20.

The gap stack again has two possible ways of slanting. The linebacker can slant right while the lineman slants left, or vice versa. What we assume is that the slant maneuver from the "gap stack" will be attacking the nose of the two blockers involved. In other words, if the stack is in the guard-tackle gap, these two linemen can expect to have a defender "on" them after the ball is snapped. The diagram depicts what we expect the defense to do. (See Diagram 4-21.)

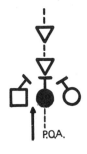

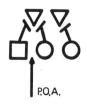

DIAGRAM 4-17

1. Right guard must block the man on, according to his second rule.
2. The right tackle assumes that a man will end up in his inside gap, and he is blocking according to his first priority: playside.
3. The center blocks according to his first rule also since there is no defender on or over.
4. The result is similar to the blocking pattern against the gap defense.

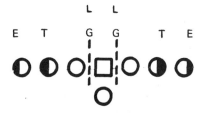

DIAGRAM 4-18: CENTER-GUARD GAP STACK.

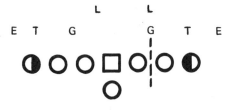

DIAGRAM 4-19: GUARD-TACKLE GAP STACK.

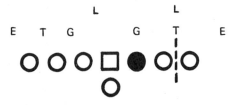

DIAGRAM 4-20: TACKLE-END GAP STACK.

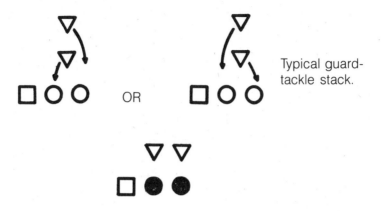

Typical guard-tackle stack.

This is the actual way we assume the gap stack will end up.

DIAGRAM 4-21

Since this type of stack could result in a stunt where one defender attacks the guard and the other attacks the tackle, both linemen must assume that they will have a man on them at the snap of the ball. It does not matter which defender slants into which blocker, both men must block according to their second priority against the gap stack, i.e., block the man "on." In order to insure that the blockers make the correct initial step to stop the penetration of the man in the gap, we refer back to our step drill. Both the tackle and the guard will step directly toward the man in the gap. Once the stacked pair of defenders makes its move, then the blockers can pick up their one-on-one assignments. If the stack does not split, then we get a double-team block by the guard and tackle on the defensive lineman in the gap. Diagrams 4-22, 4-23, 4-24 show how the blocking pattern forms.

It should be obvious that we could block the stacked defensive alignments with special types of blocking, such as the cross blocking

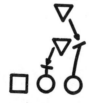

DIAGRAM 4-22

Both the guard and tackle step toward man in the gap; guard picks up inside charger, tackle picks up outside charger.

DIAGRAM 4-23

Same step results in guard still picking up inside charger and tackle picking up outside man.

DIAGRAM 4-24

The initial step puts both blockers in a position to double-team the defender even with no stunt.

outlined in Chapter 2, but these simple rules should also prove that elaborate and sophisticated techniques are not usually necessary if you are willing to analyze the defense and take away its advantages with sound one-on-one blocking and simple, consistent rules. The diagrams that follow show blocking patterns against defenses using both types of stacks. Check for yourself to see whether or not the blocking rules are being observed by every lineman. (See Diagrams 4-25, 4-26, 4-27.)

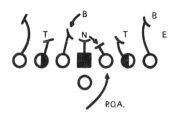

DIAGRAM 4-25: THE 5-3 STACKED DEFENSE.

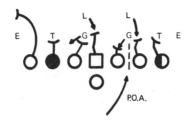

DIAGRAM 4-26: THE 6-2 GAP STACK DEFENSE.

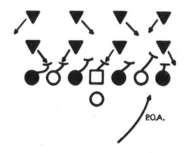

DIAGRAM 4-27: THE 4-4 STACKED DEFENSE.

BLOCKING RULES FOR SPECIAL PLAYS

In accordance with our terminology, special plays are those plays that require one or more linemen to pull out of the line to execute their blocks at the point of attack. In our system special plays are traps, sweeps, and pitch-outs. The blocking rules will vary slightly in plays of this type for the simple reason that on these plays, one or more of the interior linemen will not be in his regular position at the snap of the ball. The blocking rules for special plays are as follows:

Onside Linemen

1. Check-block for the pulling lineman next to you.
2. Block first gap away from the P.O.A.
3. Block the man on.
4. Block the man over.
5. Block backside.

Backside Linemen

Block exactly as you would for the "straight" plays, that is:

1. Playside gap.
2. On.
3. Over.
4. Backside.

The only change is in the blocking of the onside linemen because the special play makes a check block necessary (see Chapter 3). Diagrams 4-28 through 4-30 will illustrate the need for check blocking in a selection of special plays.

With the additional rule and these three examples, we can now see how the blocking patterns would develop against specific defenses for special plays. (See Diagrams 4-31, 4-32.)

You should note how a rather complex play such as a trap, can be executed without complex rules. One simple change in the blocking of the onside linemen is sufficient to compensate for the pulling blocker.

Through careful study of our special plays and the various defensive sets, the rule change for onside linemen became necessary. It is a simple change and easy to remember. The one thing that helps linemen remember the difference between straight plays and special plays is the name of the play, such as dive, trap, sweep, counter, and so on. Coupled with the hole numbering system, the linemen are more than blockers, they become intelligent thinkers and are able to analyze the reasons for blocking for specific plays in specific ways.

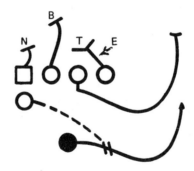

DIAGRAM 4-28: THE PITCH-OUT.

The tight end will check block for the pulling tackle.

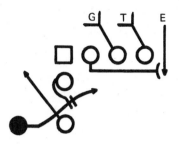

DIAGRAM 4-29: THE TRAP.

The onside tackle and end must check block for the pulling guard.

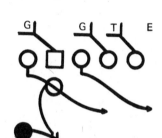

DIAGRAM 4-30: THE SWEEP.

The center, tackle and end are check blocking for the pulling guards.

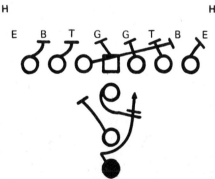

DIAGRAM 4-31: THE TRAP AT THE 4 HOLE VS. GAP 8.

1. Onside linemen block according to first priority: check block. Thus, center will check for pulling guard.

2. Right side of line then blocks according to second rule, i.e., block first gap away from P.O.A.
3. Backside linemen block according to their regular rules which has all of them blocking their third priority: playside.

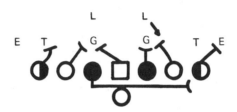

DIAGRAM 4-32:P TRAP AT THE 4 HOLE VS. 6-2 STACK.

1. Onside linemen are right end, tackle, guard and center. Each is blocking according to his first priority for a special play: "Block first gap away from the P.O.A."
2. Backside linemen are the left tackle and end, and they are blocking according to their third priority: playside; since no defender is on or over.

ADVANTAGES

The summary of this introduction to rule blocking is best presented in a list of the advantages of using such a system.

1. The consistency of the rules is guaranteed, since they are listed as priorities, not exceptions.
2. The rules can be used for all plays, straight as well as special, against all defenses, short yardage as well as open field.
3. The offensive line can use its rules against a defense it has never seen and still block it consistently.
4. Coaches can work longer on teaching fundamental blocking and not on teaching defensive alignments. All that needs to be learned are:
   a. Hole numbering.
   b. What play name means, i.e., straight or special.
   c. The blocking rules themselves.

5. The time required to teach this system is less than most others.

6. As a blocking system it may be used for any type of offense, wishbone, winged-T, pro-set, or unbalanced-line.

7. The rules encourage the linemen to seal off penetration by nature of the order of the priorities.

8. A defense that shifts, stacks or slants can not confuse the blockers who have learned this system.

9. Detailed scouting reports concerning the defensive alignments are not necessary. If scouts are difficult to come by, this is a tremendous advantage.

10. If, in any particular season, good offensive linemen are scarce, the straight blocking rules will accommodate weaknesses in the offensive line. Many teams are not blessed with the luxury of two fine pulling guards and they must therefore run all their plays with one-on-one blocking. This system is made for such a situation.

There are systems of blocking that teach the linemen to count the defensive personnel in order to find their assignments; there are systems of blocking that teach the linemen to block specific areas rather than specific men; there are systems of blocking that are different for every single play; and, finally there is the system that we offer here that combines every good aspect of all the other systems and adds simplicity and consistency to each and every offensive play. In the next chapter, we suggest a way to sophisticate these rules that might appeal to coaches who have the advantage of two-platoon players and can work with their offensive linemen daily.

CHAPTER 5

The Call System of Offensive Line Play

In this, the final chapter pertaining to blocking techniques for the running game, we offer you a sophisticated method for blocking all defenses while at the same time utilizing the best possible block type to accomplish the task. The types of blocks that will be involved in the calls have already been discussed and taught; therefore, we will not elaborate on the techniques of each block again, but rather on the call system itself, its usage and advantages. Call blocking is not new to all coaches, but it may very well be revolutionary when used in high school football. The reason for this statement is simply that we hope to convince you that this system can be implemented even in programs where two-platoon football is impossible. Since we advocate simplicity throughout our line play techniques, it is once again part and parcel of the "call system." As in the case of the rule blocking we offered in Chapter 4, the call system requires that certain prerequisites be satisfied. The terminology offered in the next section provides the base for these prerequisites.

TERMINOLOGY

Thorough understanding as well as memorization of the following terms will facilitate learning the call system:

The Call Men: Those offensive linemen responsible for calling the type of block to be used.

The Mike Call: The call that requires man-on-man blocking. (Man-on-man = mike.)

Fold Call: The call that requires a cross block with the outside lineman stepping first and the inside man going around behind.

Bingo Call: The call that requires a cross block with the inside man going first and the outside man stepping around behind.

Pinch Call: The call that requires a double-team block.

Wedge Call: The call that requires two blockers to converge on one defender, or on one area as in the case of a gap-stack.

THEORY

Theoretically, call blocking is another way of defeating the opponent who uses multiple defenses or makes drastic adjustments on the field. If the offense is successful in running a particular play off tackle, it wants to be able to continue running this play no matter what defense is thrown up to defend against it. Since many plays now in use call for a specific type of block at the point of attack, teams that use multiple defensive alignments are able to adjust and prevent that blocking type. Consequently, the offense must either discard the play or take valuable time to adjust its blocking. Consider the off-tackle play diagrammed below. The play calls for a double-team block at the 4 hole and, as Diagram 5-1 clearly shows, the play will be successful against the 5-2 defense.

After giving up big yardage, the defense wises-up and makes a slight adjustment to its off-tackle position. The adjustment may be in the form of changing the 5-2 alignment to a wide-tackle alignment, as in Diagram 5-2. Note how this change eliminates any possibility of a double-team block at the point of attack.

An offensive team whose blocking rules are so fixed that any adjustment would require a time-out or even rejection of the play as in this example, could stand to learn the theory of the call system. With the call system a designated lineman at the point of attack would be able to call for a specific kind of a block when faced with a specific kind of defense. In the case of the same off-tackle play vs. the 5-2 defense, the call man would call "pinch" in order to get the double-team block with his end. When the offense comes over the ball the next time to run the same play and the defense has switched to the wide-tackle setup, the call man now calls "mike," which tells the end that the double-team block is off and that man-on-man blocking will be used. This way the blocking is adjusted immediately at the line of scrimmage and the play can continue to be run against the ever-changing alignments. In the diagrams that follow, the power play is run against three different defenses. Each time the call is changed at the line of scrimmage and the play is run at the same point of attack, but with blocking types that accommodate the defense. (See Diagrams 5-3, 5-4, 5-5.)

This concludes the explanation of the theory of the call style of blocking. Now we will proceed to the actual breakdown of how the system works.

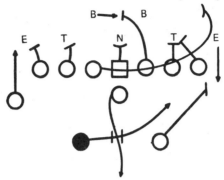

DIAGRAM 5-1

Off-tackle power play vs. 5-2 defense with double-team block at the point of attack.

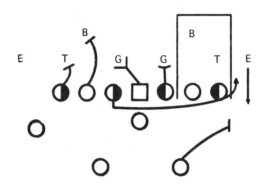

DIAGRAM 5-2

The same off-tackle power play vs. wide-tackle adjustment. The double-team between tackle and end is taken away.

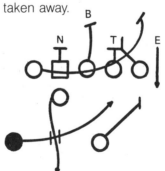

DIAGRAM 5-3: POWER PLAY VS THE 5-2 DEFENSE.

The call between tackle and end is "pinch."

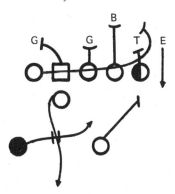

DIAGRAM 5-4

The power play again, only this time against the wide-tackle defense. The call between tackle and end in this case is "mike," to get man-on-man blocking instead of the double-team.

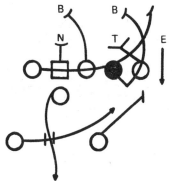

DIAGRAM 5-5

Once again the power play is run to the 4 hole, this time vs. the 5-3 stack. The call is "fold" so that the tackle and end can pick up the stack and the play is still sound.

HOW THE CALL SYSTEM WORKS

Two facets of the call system that are vital have already been discussed. First, our blocking rules are called by the priority system as outlined in Chapter 4. Second, the points of attack, or holes, are numbered by gaps as shown in Diagram 5-6.

Although one might not think that this numbering system is significant, in reality it is vital to the call system. The reason for this is that any call that is made can affect only two blockers, and in order to alert the two proper blockers, the point of attack must be between them. As an example, see how Diagram 5-7 illustrates those linemen who are near each hole. Clearly, if you name a point of attack, there are always two linemen who know that they are right next to the hole.

To emphasize the need for this numbering system, let's look at another type of numbering system and see if we can accommodate the call system theory with it. (See Diagram 5-8.)

This system numbers the linemen rather than the gaps, and the confusion that comes in from this setup can be seen when we ask the question, "What two blockers are near the 5 hole? The 2 hole? The 6

DIAGRAM 5-6

Hole numbering system for call system.

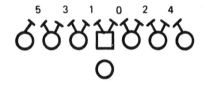

DIAGRAM 5-7

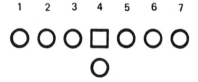

DIAGRAM 5-8

hole?" As you can see, if we were to run a play into the 6 hole for example, the right end, right tackle, and right guard are all near the hole. Thus, if a call were to be made to change the blocking, three men would have to be involved, and this would cause a great deal of confusion. I contend, therefore, that gap numbers are vital to this system, whether they are numbered in order or by evens and odds makes no difference.

DESIGNATING THE CALL MEN

The call men actually control the blocking from end to end on the offensive line. It is therefore imperative that we choose linemen who are located central to call points of attack. Through trial and error, we found that the tackles and the center would be able to call the blocking for every point of attack. Diagram 5-9 shows that the right tackle's call can be directed to himself and the right guard when a 2-hole play is called, and his call can be directed to himself and the right end when a 4-hole play is to be run.

The left tackle on the other side of the line has the same responsibility. His calls will control the left guard, himself, and the left end blocking patterns. Thus, plays run to the 3 and 5 holes can be blocked different ways by the left tackle's calls. (See Diagram 5-10.)

Finally, the 0 and 1 holes are controlled by the center. His calls will direct the right and left guard depending upon which hole is to be attacked. If the play being run is a 1-hole play, the center's call will be directed to himself and the left guard. (See Diagram 5-11.)

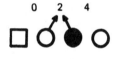

DIAGRAM 5-9

The right tackle makes calls for the 2 and 4 holes, thus controlling the blocks of the right guard, himself, and the right end.

DIAGRAM 5-10

The left tackle controls the blocking of the left guard for 3-hole plays, and the blocking of the left tackle for 5-hole plays.

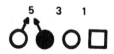

DIAGRAM 5-11

The center's calls change the blocking-types at the 1 hole for the left guard, and at the 0 hole for the right guard.

Up to this point we have the following essential ingredients for installing the call systems:

1. Terminology and code names for block types.
2. A set of one-on-one blocking rules.
3. Theoretical reason for using this system.
4. A hole numbering system to accommodate call blocking.
5. Designated call men.

Now let's assume we are in a ball game and the opponent is using multiple defenses on every play.

GAME SITUATION

The quarterback calls a play in the huddle, "30 dive, on two." The team breaks the huddle and assumes the pre-set position. While in this pre-set position, the three call men look over the defense and decide what call they want to make. Before the quarterback says "Down," a call is made by all three of the call men. The only call which has any meaning is the call made by the center, since he controls the blocking for the 0 hole. The call made by the two tackles are "dummy" calls. The dummy calls are essential so that the defense can not pick them up and react to them. Dummy calls are made on every play, regardless of whether it is a pass, run or kicking situation. In Diagrams 5-12, 5-13, and 5-14, the 30 dive is shown with several blocking schemes against several defenses.

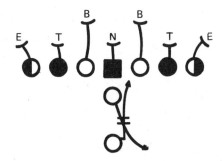

DIAGRAM 5-12: 30 DIVE VS. 5-2 REGULAR

Center calls "mike" for one-on-one blocking.

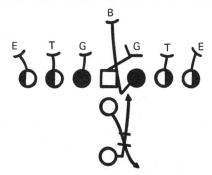

DIAGRAM 5-13: 30 DIVE VS. 6-1 PRO

Center calls "bingo" to get cross block with right guard.

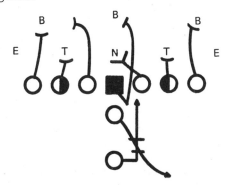

DIAGRAM 5-14: 30 DIVE VS. 5-3 IN DEFENSE

Center again calls for a cross block, only it is a fold technique that controls the 0 hole and right guard.

Since the calls that are made affect only the blocking that goes on at the point of attack, the other linemen simply block according to their rules. In each of the preceding diagrams, the linemen not involved in the call were blocking according to:

1. Playside gap
2. On
3. Over
4. Backside

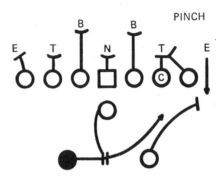

DIAGRAM 5-15: 34 SLANT VS. 5-2 REGULAR.

Tackle calls "pinch" to get double-team with his 4-hole partner, the right end.

All other linemen block according to their priorities.

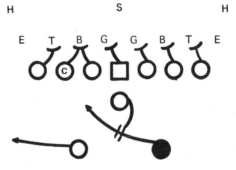

DIAGRAM 5-16: 23 QUICK VS GAP 8.

Left tackle is the call man. He calls "wedge" which gives him and the left guard a double-team at the P.O.A. Note how every defender is blocked by other blockers' use of priorities. Their third priority is in effect, playside gap.

The beauty of the call system lies in the fact that while you are getting the best possible block at the point of attack to accommodate the ever-changing defense, at the same time you are getting the most simple and consistent rule blocking everywhere else. This type of blocking system allows for sophistication as well as simplicity and consistency. Take note of the application of the regular blocking rules executed by the blockers not involved in the call as well as the types of calls being used against defensive changes. (See Diagrams 5-15, 5-16.)

At this point, you should have some questions about the ability of the linemen to know what call to make. On paper it looks very good, but how does a high school lineman know the difference between using the mike and the pinch call? Or more difficult yet, the fold versus the bingo call? The next section will be devoted to answering these questions.

HOW TO TEACH THE USE OF CALLS

In order to be a great offensive lineman, a player must understand defensive alignments, strategy, and techniques. Although it may not always be part of the coach's philosophy, we insist that every lineman learn a defensive as well as an offensive line position. Through some practical experience, insight into the actions of the defensive linemen can be gained. The first process in teaching the way calls are to be used is to teach the offensive linemen how to recognize the defense in front of them. We break the multiple defenses into each blocker's position area and then show them what alignments are possible and what calls can be made. We never refer to a defense as odd or even, because we are only concerned with how the defense is aligned at the point of attack. Once the blockers learn the possible alignments, we show them how they are similar, and eventually, we categorize defensive alignments according to our blocking calls. For example, there is absolutely no difference between a 5-2 alignment and a 6-1 alignment over the center and right guard. All that has happened is that the linebacker who was over the guard in the 5-2, came down to an on position on the guard and the nose-guard in the 5-2 dropped back to a middle linebacker. Since this type of change does not affect the point of attack, say the 0 hole, the blocking type may be the same. The changes that are of major concern are those that move a defender from an on or over position, to a gap or stacked position. In the chart that follows, we have diagrammed the possible defensive alignments that the right tackle and right end will see, and the possible calls that could block these alignments. (See chart, Diagram 5-17.)

For further simplification, the reader should note that every defensive alignment, with the exception of the stacks, can be blocked with mike blocking. Therefore, if you wanted to keep the calls to a minimum, you would merely teach your linemen to recognize stacked defenses and the calls that you want them to use for them.

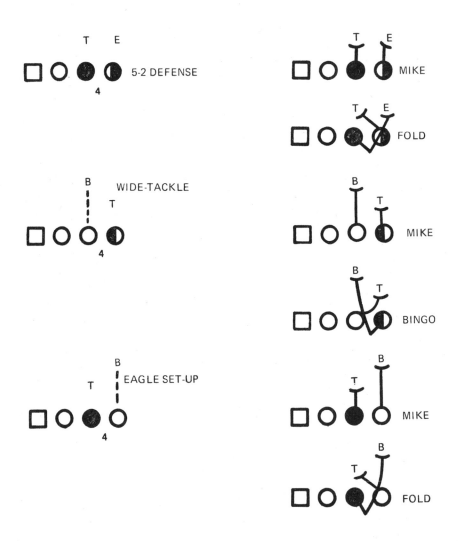

POSSIBLE DEFENSIVE ALIGNMENTS
AT THE 4 HOLE

POSSIBLE CALLS FOR
RIGHT TACKLE TO USE

5-2 DEFENSE

MIKE

FOLD

WIDE-TACKLE

MIKE

BINGO

EAGLE SET-UP

MIKE

FOLD

DIAGRAM 5-17

POSSIBLE DEFENSIVE ALIGNMENTS
AT THE 4 HOLE

POSSIBLE CALLS FOR
RIGHT TACKLE TO USE

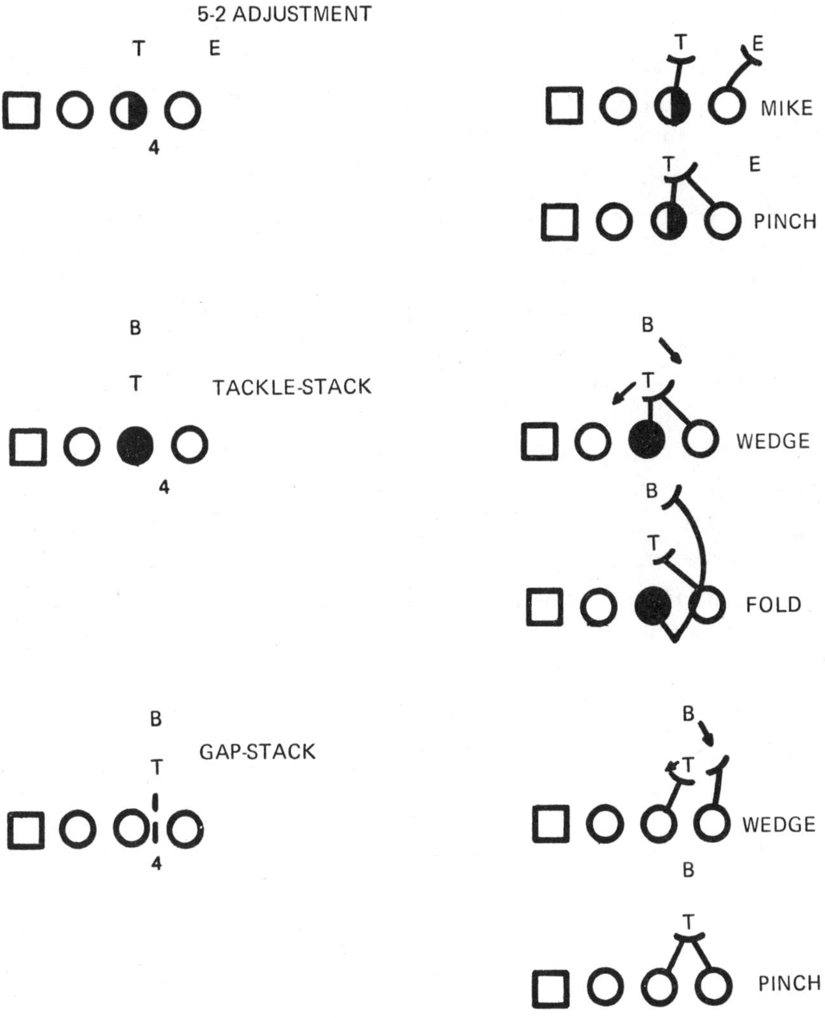

5-2 ADJUSTMENT

TACKLE-STACK

GAP-STACK

DIAGRAM 5-17 (CONT.)

Similar charts can be prepared for the tackle and
guard, and the center and guard.

ADVANTAGES OF THE CALL SYSTEM

As a final tribute to the call system, we offer you these advantages of its use as we have found them in the past years:

1. It enables the offensive team to utilize the best possible block at the point of attack on every play against every defensive alignment.
2. It teaches the linemen how to play football. They are no longer considered "stupid" linemen.
3. Scouting reports need not be so detailed, and if they are not detailed enough, the call system will still accommodate the defensive sets, even when the linemen have not been exposed to them previously.
4. Call blocking is an extra advantage that the blocker has over the defender.
5. It is the coach's answer to multiple defenses with a certain amount of sophistication, simplicity and consistency.
6. The complete offensive game plan may be used regardless of defensive adjustments. No plays need be discarded.
7. Memorization of what block type is to be used for which play, is no longer necessary. The blockers will determine their own blocking.
8. Teaching time is cut to a minimum, leaving more time for the coach to perfect fundamental blocking techniques.
9. It allows for on-the-field adjustments to be made by those people closest to the situation.
10. It gives part of the game to the players, much as play-calling gives the game to the quarterback; consequently, player morale improves.

CONCLUDING REMARKS

The running play sets up every other possibility in offensive football, and without a substantial running attack, the passing game will be sporadic, to say the least. The techniques have been presented here in a cumulative manner, indicating that one precedes the other, and so, having established a sound running game, we proceed to put the ball in the air.

CHAPTER **6**

Drop-Back Pass Blocking

Drop-back passing is a vital part of every offensive system. Any coach who uses drop-back passing must spend a great deal of time perfecting and disciplining his receivers on their pattern routes and his quarterback on his drop-back action as well as his ability to read defenses. In these two areas alone, the coach will spend at least half of his practice time. Yet blocking for this form of the passing game involves far more technique and requires far greater skill and talent than does running of pass routes or catching the ball. Drop-back pass protection is an art, and as an art it demands precision, balance, agility, intelligence, technique, and an equal amount of practice time spent with receivers and quarterbacks. The techniques and coaching points offered in this chapter represent a compilation of more than 15 years of personal offensive line playing experience, and 13 years of offensive line coaching experience. Any coach who has searched for teaching aids in this area of the game or who has looked for special techniques that will afford him the best pass protection possible, would do well to read and re-read this chapter.

A PASSING PHILOSOPHY

The team that uses the drop-back pass as an offensive weapon must also have a particular philosophy about the passing game. By "philosophy" we also mean "reason." The question, "Why do we drop back in order to throw the football?" must be answered. We use the drop-back pass sparingly, but we have definite reasons for using it at all, and we find that those reasons also support our philosophy on the overall passing game.

First, the formation changes that are made to accommodate the receivers in their execution of pass patterns for a multitude of routes can also help disguise your running game. For example, if you split an end and a flanker whenever you want to drop back and pass, this will spread out the defensive secondary. By spreading the defense with a passing formation, you make all your running plays more threatening since the secondary must defend against the wide receivers first and often lose sight of their interior keys. Because of this, it follows that our particular philosophy would favor the running game first, while using the drop-back passing attack as a complement to it. Many other coaches tend to follow the opposite philosophy, which places primary importance on the passing game while using the running play as a change-up.

Second, by passing from the drop-back action from a number of different formations, you may force the defensive secondary into a variation of its normal coverages, which leads to confusion. Once this begins to happen, you can make the job easier for the passer because he will be able to pick up weaknesses in the coverage and isolate one primary target. This reduces the possibility for interceptions or quarterback sacks.

Third, the variations in formations automatically provide your offensive running game with the multiplicity that confounds the line and linebackers, which in turn makes your offensive linemen's jobs easier.

Finally, in the event that a drop-back pass is absolutely necessary, say for instance in a two-minute drill at the end of the half or at the end of the game, the bomb becomes more effective since the defense is merely guessing at what you are going to do when your team sets up over the ball. Whatever your philosophy is on the passing game, the coaching techniques employed by all involved must never be short-changed, regardless of whether you throw four times per game or forty-four times per game. If each pass is to be executed properly, then these are the techniques that should be taught.

THE STANCE

As in the running game, the stance becomes the first major technique that will determine whether or not the block will be well executed. In no way should the stance be altered to accommodate pass blocking but must remain the same as that stance used in all situations. Offensive linemen should be taught to respect their defensive counterparts enough never to cheat in their stances, for any good defender will pick up that change and read the play every time. Drop-back pass blocking is one technique that will certainly tell whether or not the blocker has a perfect stance. When blocking for the running play, a blocker will not be hampered by a stance that causes him to have his weight too far forward, but if he keeps this stance in an attempt to pass block, he will be in deep trouble. The stance should be such that the weight is perfectly balanced so that the blocker can move in any direction with maximum quickness, power, and balance.

THE TWO-POINT STANCE

The very best position to start from in drop-back pass blocking is the two-point stance. There are definite advantages to the two-point stance in pass blocking. First, in this stance the blocker's head and eyes are up and he is afforded maximum visibility. In cases when drop-back passing is imminent and the defense is stunting, looping, or blitzing in some way, visibility is vital. Second, the blocker does not have to set himself in a balanced position on the snap of the ball, he is already up and prepared to make contact in a good hitting position. Third, this two-point stance gives the blocker more time to see how the defender is charging without back peddling right away. If the defender charges to the inside, the most dangerous route as far as the blocker is concerned, then the blocker is already prepared to protect this route. Finally, this stance practically eliminates those embarrassing times when a quick defender out-charges your blocker and knocks him over on his backside while your blocker is attempting to set up to pass block.

DISGUISING THE DROP-BACK PASS

One might wonder about the contradiction here: Doesn't the two-point stance give away the fact that we are going to pass? The answer is no. Furthermore, it will add to the disguise of the drop-back pass if used when the offensive team breaks the huddle and the offensive linemen set themselves in a pre-set position, i.e., the two-point stance. This is done prior to every play, regardless of whether it is run or pass. On most occasions, the quarterback will make signal calls, a set call, or even a check-off call, but on some call the linemen will get down into their offensive stance. However, once the defense gets used to this routine, they will not actually prepare themselves to rush or stunt or loop, or do whatever it is they have planned to do, until the linemen are in their three-point stance. Therefore, when we are going to throw a drop-back pass, we will snap the ball on the quarterback's first sound while the linemen are still in their pre-set stance. By doing this we feel we give ourselves the following advantages:

1. It puts the blocker in perfect pass protection posture instantly.

2. Defensive maneuvers in the line are negated by the offense's quick start. The defense loses the element of surprise.

3. Due to the quickness of the snap, the defense loses its quickness, that is so vital in pass rushing.

It is imperative that the blocker never tip-off the defender by any variation in the way he pre-sets himself on each and every play, run or pass. The quarterback's cadence must also remain the same and with a constant rhythm and sequence. In this way, the two-point stance will never give a drop-back pass away to the defense, and at the same time it will give the blocker the best possible advantage over the defender.

THE CORRECT INITIAL STEP

Before any lineman can become an effective pass blocker, he must be fully aware of the many defensive tactics that are available to his opponent. Once aware of the defensive tactics for pass rushing, the blocker can prepare himself and use some techniques of his own to protect the passer. The first tactic used by many defensive pass rushers is a slanting charge to the inside of the blocker. This path is the shortest route the defender can take and it becomes the most dangerous to the blocker. The inside route must be taken away from the defender immediately. This can be accomplished very easily by teaching the pass blocker to take one simple step each and every time he blocks for a drop-back pass.

On the quarterback's signal to put the ball in play, each and every offensive linemen must take a lateral jab-step toward the inside. This initial step must be lateral and not backward, as a backward step will create a gap between the two neighboring linemen. Also, this initial step need not be any more than six to eight inches as it is merely a position step. If this initial step is taken quickly and correctly, it will discourage the defender from shooting to the inside and it will force him either to run straight ahead or take the outside route. In either case, the blocker has taken the inside path away from the defender and forced him to go where he can be blocked the way the blocker wishes. The blocking scheme showing the initial step as it should be taken by the interior linemen is shown in Diagram 6-1.

The technique is completed when the blocker sets his other foot. Having completed the inside jab-step which is a position step, the blocker now drops his outside foot back on an angle of 45 degrees with the line of scrimmage. This completed, the initial step cuts off the inside route and actually "suckers" the defender into charging to the outside. All this technique is accomplished with little or no contact between the blocker and the defender. The total picture of the initial step is seen in Diagrams 6-1 through 6-3.

The offensive center represents the middle-man in the formation of the pass protection unit, and as such he does not need either the jab-step or the drop-step technique in drop-back passing blocking. His

R.F. R.F.   L.F.   L.F.

DIAGRAM 6-1: THE JAB-STEP (PHASE 1).
Initial step to the inside.

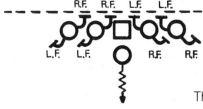

R.F. R.F. L.F.   L.F.

L.F. L.F.   R.F.   R.F.

DIAGRAM 6-2: PHASE 2.
The jab-step and drop-step combined.

DIAGRAM 6-3: PHASE 3.
The protection cup formed by initial step.

initial steps must first get him into the correct two-point stance for balance and all-around blocking posture. The center's snap should be of sufficient force to enable him to get up into a hitting position quickly. From here he will drop-step straight back or as the defender playing over him dictates. This blocker should keep his shoulders parallel with the line of scrimmage for as long as possible before looking to either side for a man to block lest a linebacker loop up the middle on a blitz. The next phase of the drop-back pass block involves the keys. These are the fundamentals of drop-back pass blocking.

THE FUNDAMENTALS OF DROP-BACK PASS BLOCKING

It goes without saying that the first and foremost fundamental is a sound blocking stance, and this has already been described as the two-point stance. The second fundamental has also been described and that is getting into the proper position to begin blocking the defender. Having accomplished this much, the blocker must now be prepared to make contact with the defender and keep him away from the quarter-back without going downfield past the neutral zone. We can best teach the reader these techniques in the same way we teach our assistant coaches and the players themselves. We will list each technique and then add a full description for each one:

1. *Foot-fire.* In order to maintain the proper hitting position and absolute balance throughout contact, the blocker must keep his feet moving constantly from the time the ball is snapped until the time the play is blown dead. We refer to this action of the feet as foot-fire and we emphasize it constantly. The athlete must move his feet rapidly about shoulder width, on the balls of his feet, and with short, choppy motions. As soon as this action stops, the athlete will instinctively lean or lunge at the defender and fall to his knees. Foot-fire, when executed properly, insures that the blocker will remain on his feet throughout all contact made with the defender.

2. *Clench fists and hands high.* We combine these two techniques because they both involve the hands. Clenching the fists insures that the blocker will not grab the defender and be guilty of holding. By keeping the hands high, we stress the use of hands and forearms as a shield against the blows delivered by the defender. Much in the same way that a boxer will use his hands and arms to parry the blows delivered by his opponent, the pass blocker should keep his hands and arms high to parry the hand and arm tactics used by the defender. These techniques include side shots to the shoulder and head area of the blocker, which, if delivered with enough force, could knock the blocker off balance. By anticipating these blows and defending against them, the blocker can maintain his balance and continue to be an effective part of the pass protection unit. The blocker must remember that while he may use his hands and arms to protect himself, he may not use them to stop a defender from passing him.

3. *Use proper contact surface.* The proper surface with which the blocker should make contact with the pass rusher is generally deter-mined by the nature of the pass play, but for drop-back action we insist that the blocker keep the defender right in front of him. Contact should then only be made with the hands. The type of contact sustained in pass blocking is relatively free of the same kind of force one encounters in one-on-one blocking for the running game. Furthermore, the eyes are

nothing more than an aiming or sighting device that helps the blocker keep the defensive man in front of him. With the eyes and hands the blocker should meet the charging defender and make contact with him about chest high. The hands are better than the forearms as a point of contact in that they enable the blocker to get a quicker and better feel for the way the defender changes the path of his charge toward the quarterback. If the pass rusher hits the blocker straight on and then slides quickly to the right, the blocker will feel the extra pressure on his hand and will be able to react properly more quickly than if he used his forearms as a contact surface. It should be noted, however, that if the blocker uses his hands to prevent the pass rusher from getting past him, or if he overextends his hands, he will again be guilty of holding. The proper technique for using the hands requires only that the blocker keep his elbows close to his body.

4. *Hit-retreat-cut.* The passer requires at least seven seconds for a normal drop-back pass, and in order to get this kind of time, the blocker should avoid trying to maintain constant contact with the defender. If he does try to maintain contact, he may be overrun, thrown to the side, or out-maneuvered by some fancy footwork or hand tactic. To avoid this possibility, we teach a hit-retreat-cut tactic which gives us the necessary time for effective pass protection.

a. *Hit.* In this phase, the blocker merely squares himself in front of the defender and hits him squarely in the middle of his chest. This hit is only forceful enough to stop the rusher's forward progress long enough for the blocker to get away from him and retreat.

b. *Retreat.* The blocker quickly resets himself in a hitting position by retreating to avoid being grabbed or out-maneuvered by the defender. His retreat should be deep enough to get clearly away from the defender but not so deep that he interferes with the passer. The retreating action, along with the hitting action, must be accomplished with constant foot action or foot-fire technique.

c. *Cut.* Once the blocker has retreated, enough time has elapsed so that the rusher must commit himself to one route. At this point the defender is hell-bent for the quarterback, and is probably at full speed. When this situation presents itself, I teach my blockers to cut the defender and take him cleanly off his feet. The cut block must be executed perfectly, or else the defender will recover and still make the play. To cut the defender, the blocker will keep his head up and his feet constantly firing in place, with no forward or backward movement. As the defender gets right on top of the blocker, the blocker throws his head to the outside and his shoulders into the rusher's thighs. This cutting action is intended to take the defender down completely, and also has the advantage of bringing his hands down so that he can't block the pass or the passer's vision by simply extending his hands.

The hit-retreat-cut technique may be altered in many ways. It may be shortened to simple cut-blocking, excellent for quick passes that require no time at all. Also, this technique may be extended to hit-retreat-hit-retreat-cut to insure that the blocker does not cut the defender too soon. In any case, we feel that the cut phase should be included in drop-back blocking techniques since it lends itself nicely to those linemen who are not exceptionally big or strong but are continually playing opposite bigger opponents. It is also a much easier way to learn pass blocking, since many high school programs do not have the time or the coaches to spend all kinds of time teaching pass protection of the quality used in professional football.

TYPES OF DROP-BACK PASS BLOCKING

There are three types of drop-back pass blocking styles that can be used. The coach may select one specific type and use it exclusively, or he may teach all three types and give his blockers the privilege of calling what type they will use as they discover the way the defenders put on the rush. The determining factors will be coaching time available, ability of the linemen, and overall passing philosophy. The first and most common type of drop-back pass protection is the cup protection and is outlined below along with man-for-man pass protection, and a more recent type that we call the slide technique.

Cup Protection

This type of pass protection is perhaps the most common and the easiest to teach. Beyond the coaching of the jab- and drop-step techniques, cup protection requires little else in coaching. The main point to stress to the offensive blocker in this type of pass protection is that the defender must be kept to the outside of the middle zone where the quarterback is setting up to pass. Once the initial steps have been taken and the blocker has closed off the inside rushing lane, he may keep the defender outside in two ways:

1. *Aggressive blocking.* The blocker attacks the defender and may use any one of the one-on-one blocking techniques described in Chapter 1.

Diagram 6-4 shows that the blocker is driving the defender away from the quarterback's zone and is, in effect, blocking him as though it were a running play. The blocker in this type of protection actually "suckers" the defender into a position where he can be blocked from the side.

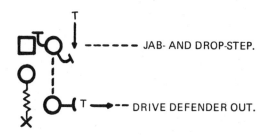

DIAGRAM 6-4

Aggressive blocking for drop-back pass protection.

2. *Hit-retreat or shuffle technique.* The pass blocker again takes his initial steps to seal off the inside lane, but in order to keep the pass rusher outside, he will hit and retreat and continue to do this protecting the inside zone occupied by the passer. The blocker shuffles his feet laterally as he hits the defender and retreats, but his contact with the defender is only forceful enough to keep him from penetrating to the inside, not forceful enough to knock him down. As a last resort, the blocker may cut the rusher's legs out from under him. Diagram 6-5 depicts the imaginary line along which the pass blocker must shuffle in order to keep the defender out of the passer's zone.

Cup protection has its greatest advantage when the two setbacks in the offensive formation join the blocking unit. This setup affords maximum pass protection as it accounts for all defenders on the line as well as any linebackers that may blitz. The disadvantage occurs when the offense wants to send more than three receivers out for a pass. When this occurs another type of pass protection should be used. Diagram 6-6 shows the formation of the entire blocking cup. Cup protection is based on area blocking philosophy, which simply means that if there is no defender in a given area, the blocker will have no responsibility other than to act as a helper or to beware of a blitzing linebacker. (See Diagram 6-7.)

DIAGRAM 6-5

The inside position step forces the rusher to go outside the blocker. The blocker keeps the defender out of the passer's zone by shuffling, hitting and retreating gradually.

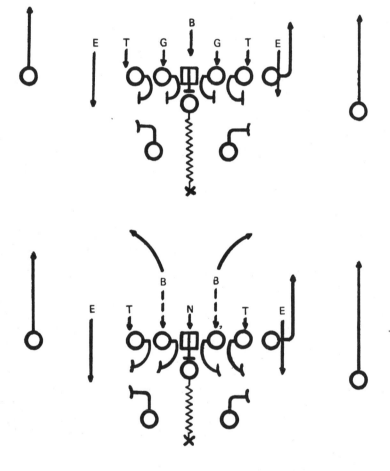

DIAGRAM 6-6

Cup blocking scheme vs. two different defensive sets.

The disadvantage of cup blocking is clearly seen when a fourth receiver is put into the pattern. Note how the defensive left end has a clear shot at the passer. A different type of pass protection is needed here.

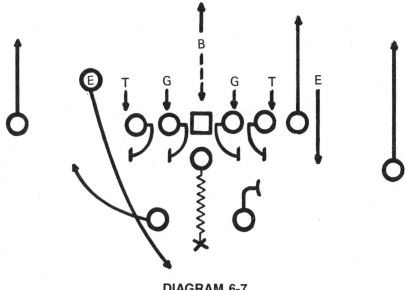

DIAGRAM 6-7

Man-for-Man Pass Blocking

Cup protection is a very conservative means by which dropback passing may be protected. In order to open up the options of receivers to throw to, and to sophisticate the passing game, coaches may go to the man-for-man protection. In this type of protection, each blocker is assigned a specific man, and he must block that man no matter where he goes. The rules for man-for-man protection would be as follows:

Center: Block the nose-guard in an odd defense; if no down lineman is playing head up on you, drop back and block the defensive end to your right or left. You will block left when the left halfback is in the pattern, and you will block right when the right halfback is in the pattern. Coach's play-calling usually includes some key that tells the center which way to block. (See Diagram 6-8.)

Guards: The guards are responsible for the first down lineman to appear off the center. They are never responsible for the nose-guard, nor are they responsible for a blitzing linebacker as they were in the cup type of protection. (See Diagrams 6-9, 6-10.)

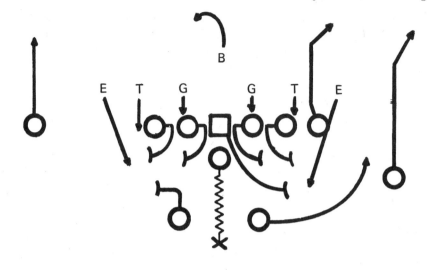

DIAGRAM 6-8

Center's pass block vs. even man defense with right halfback in the pass pattern. All assignments are man-for-man.

Tackles: The tackles are responsible for the second down lineman to show off the center. In both the odd and even defensive alignments they will be blocking the biggest, strongest and quickest lineman on the opposing team. Therefore, teams that use the man-for-man type of pass protection should select their offensive tackles keeping this in mind. (See Diagrams 6-11, 6-12.)

Man-for-man pass protection is best used against a defense that only uses four defensive linemen to rush the passer. As soon as the defense rushes more than four people, the offense must keep one or more backs in to help block. Blitzing is very effective against the team that employs man-for-man pass protection exclusively. It is very helpful to be able to send four or more receivers downfield in a passing situation, and in such a situation man-for-man pass protection is excellent. But using this type exclusively would soon force the defense to blitz and stunt more often than normal, making your pass protection extremely weak. The final type of pass protection allows the linemen to make changes in their blocking on the line of scrimmage without affecting the backfield blocking or the kind of pass patterns that can be used. We call this "slide" blocking.

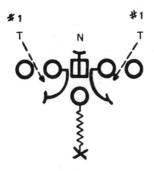

DIAGRAM 6-9

Guards' man-for-man blocking assignments vs. odd man defense.

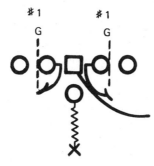

DIAGRAM 6-10

Guards' man-for-man blocking assignments vs. even man defense.

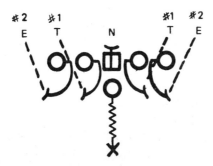

DIAGRAM 6-11

Tackles' blocking assignments in man-for-man protection vs. odd man defense.

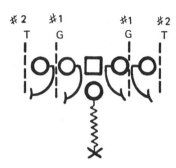

DIAGRAM 6-12

Tackles' blocking assignments in man-for-man protection vs. even man defense.

Slide Blocking for Drop-Back Passes

The act of sliding in this type of pass protection is done by the guards. They will slide down from their positions to the outside to pick up a rushing defender so long as no one has rushed over their regular positions. Before sliding to the outside, the guards will check to make certain that no linebacker is blitzing over them, for if one does blitz, the guard must block him. Using the slide technique gives you the advantages of both the cup and the man-for-man types of pass protection. On any particular pass play, one or both guards may slide, or it is possible that the defense will be such that neither guard can use the technique at all. Diagrams 6-13 and 6-14 show how and when the slide technique might be used in a number of defensive situations.

The offensive tackles will always block the man on or slightly to their outside. There is never any counting done with this type of pass protection, and it is designed to protect the middle first, the outside second. Middle blitzes should never hurt the passing game with this type of pass protection. The slide technique may also be used in the backfield. For example, if the right halfback is assigned to block the end, and the end drops off in pass defense, the halfback should then be able to slide off into the flat or hook zone for a short safety pass. (See Diagram 6-15.)

Coaches must consider every aspect of their offensive theory before choosing one of the three types of pass protection offered in this chapter. Regardless of which type of pass protection is chosen, there are certain fundamentals that are consistent. They are as follows:

1. Coach the perfect stance and pass blocking posture.
2. Coach the correct initial step to close off the inside.
3. Coach the legal use of hands, clenched fists and hands high.

4. Coach foot-fire, the rapid and constant foot movement.

5. Coach hit-retreat-cut, a series of techniques.

6. Coach rules that make for easy assignments and easy reading.

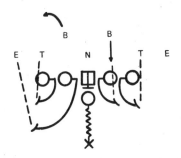

DIAGRAM 6-13

Slide blocking vs. 52 defense with one line-backer blitzing.

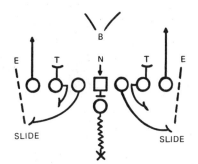

DIAGRAM 6-14

Slide blocking vs. 53 defense.

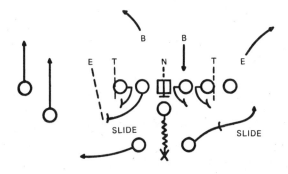

DIAGRAM 6-15

With these simple coaching points and the techniques offered here, you will see vast improvements in the overall drop-back passing game, with fewer interceptions and fewer quarterback sacks. In the following two chapters we offer some fine techniques that will enhance the effectiveness of your air attack while faking the running game.

CHAPTER 7

Sprint-Out Pass Blocking

When a team predominantly throws the football by dropping back, the defense can regulate its coverage and challenge the offense to execute properly. There is very little surprise involved in an offense that drops back each and every time it is going to throw the football. Furthermore, the coverage techniques for the defense are relatively simple against the straight drop-back passer since the defense has only to mirror the drop-back depth with its own drop-back. On the other hand, should the offensive team sprint-out to one side or another before throwing the football, the defense has to rotate toward that side as well as drop back for depth, and these two movements often leave gaping holes in the coverage zones. It is also relatively easy for the offensive team to incorporate several running plays off the sprint-out action, making coverage even more difficult for the secondary. The great advantages of sprint-out passing are enhanced when an offense employs drop-back passing as well, for these combinations keep the defense confused and uncertain as to whether it should rotate or drop back, cover pass or defend against the run. In the pages that follow we will give you the best possible techniques for blocking on the sprint-out pass.

A PASSING PHILOSOPHY

The reasons that support the "why" of the sprint-out pass are many. Since the passer must sprint to one side or another, the defense must rotate quickly so that he will not get outside the coverage zones. Moreover, as the passer sprints out, he takes the passing pocket with him and thereby forces the entire defensive secondary to move with him. This rapid rotation forces the secondary to vacate the side away from the direction of the sprint-out. Passes, screens, or draws that go back to this side are quite deadly for this reason. Another asset not found in any other style of passing is the quarterback's option to run as well as to throw. Many coaches call this type of pass a "run first—pass second" option since the secondary will more often than not hang back in expectation of the pass and leave the quarterback uncovered. The threats to the defense are many and, if more than two receivers are sent into an area on a "flood" pattern, the options are limitless. This type of passing game makes the running game more effective, while at the same time, there is not the same kind of a burden on the offensive linemen when it comes to blocking for the pass. The act of sprinting-out by the passer forces the pass rushers to go in one precise direction, and since the blockers already know which way the passer will sprint-out, they can expect the rushers to charge a specific way. The techniques of pass blocking become greatly simplified and position becomes the true key to successful sprint-out pass blocking. If your philosophy is predicated on the running game, then the sprint-out pass is an extremely good complement. Many coaches, however, will refrain from using the sprint-out pass for the simple reason that their quarterback is not a great runner. The quarterback need not be a 1,000-yard gainer in order to make the sprint-out effective, but as long as he poses some threat as a running back, the defense will have to respect him. Thus, the philosophy that holds the running game in higher esteem than the long bomb or a predominant passing attack is maintained by the sprint-out pass.

THE STANCE

We can never say enough about the necessity for the proper stance in all phases of offensive line play, and the sprint-out pass is no different. However, unlike the drop-back pass that requires the blocker to drop back as he makes contact with the defender, the sprint-out pass does not require a retreat. All that is required is that the blocker get good position on the pass rusher and influence him away from the quarterback's route. For this reason the blocker does not have to be set in a two-point stance but may move easily from his regular set position to a comfortable blocking posture. This is not to say that the same technique for starting a play in the pre-set position could not be used, for starting from the two-point stance would certainly not hamper the blocker. Thus, the quick count while blockers are still in their pre-set stance is still an effective surprise weapon.

DISGUISING THE SPRINT-OUT PASS

Because it is difficult to throw a long drop-back pass from a tight formation, many times a team will also split an end and spread out their intended receivers. The sprint-out pass, however, can be thrown from any formation, tight or spread, since the passer's sprint-out gives the receivers enough time to get well into their pass routes. Since tight formations are often associated with running plays, this would be one way to disguise a sprint-out pass. Another way is to use men in motion, something not often used in drop-back passes. The men in motion may be used as blockers for the sprint-out passer, as decoys for the running game, or they may be used as safety valves in the actual pass pattern. Greater still as a disguise is the very nature of the sprint-out itself. Since the passer can either run or throw the ball, the options make it possible for the sprint-out to be used at all times, for long yardage as well as short, inside the opponent's ten-yard line or inside your own, on first down or on fourth. The greatest disguise is the sprint-out game itself. Finally, since the offensive linemen do not have to retreat to block as in the cup or man-for-man styles of drop-back passing, the defensive secondary is unable to read their keys quickly enough to successfully defend all the options that are open to the sprint-out team.

THE CORRECT INITIAL STEPS

The initial steps taken by the offensive linemen reflect the same steps taken by the passer on his sprint-out route. If the passer is to sprint-out to the right, he must step with his right foot first and in the intended direction. Since this action will draw the defenders to the right also, it is essential that the offensive linemen anticipate this step and move in that direction as quickly as possible. Everyone on the offense knows which way the sprint-out will go and their initial steps will put them in the best possible position to meet the defender. Furthermore, the defense's reaction to the direction of the sprint-out is not immediate, and if the offense takes its initial position step properly, it will have a tremendous blocking angle on the pass rushers. The direction of the sprint-out sets the stage for the initial steps taken by each blocking lineman. The linemen are then divided into two categories, the onside linemen and the backside linemen. If the sprint-out is left, the onside linemen are the center, left guard, and left tackle, while the backside linemen are the right guard and the right tackle. If the sprint-out is to the right, then the center, right guard, and right tackle are considered onside, while the left guard and the left tackle are backside. The distinction must be made here because after the initial step is taken, the interior linemen will block with different techniques depending on whether they are onside or backside linemen. These techniques are the basic fundamentals of the sprint-out pass block.

THE FUNDAMENTALS OF SPRINT-OUT PASS BLOCKING

When a forward pass is thrown, certain rules govern the behavior of the interior linemen which prohibit them from going beyond the neutral zone. Violation of this rule makes the lineman guilty of a fifteen-yards penalty as an ineligible receiver. When a quarterback decides to run the football after seeing that a drop-back pass will not be successful, the linemen will often cross the neutral zone and go downfield to block for the scrambling quarterback. Since nothing but pass was planned in the huddle, the quarterback's decision to run catches everyone off guard and may result in a big gain or, should the quarterback decide to pass after all, it may result in an ineligible receiver downfield in the form of an overzealous lineman. The very nature of the sprint-out pass allows for the option of running or passing without the possibility of an ineligible receiver. Let's say that the sprint-out is to the right. In this case, the offensive linemen will all take a position step and drop-step to the right to get position on the defender. The onside linemen, center, right guard, and right tackle, will block aggressively without retreating and in the same manner as an area block. Since they are onside, they know that the quarterback will sprint past them quickly and that a quick, aggressive block is all that is needed so that the quarterback may get past the defenders on that side of the line. After taking their position step, it would be perfectly fitting for the inside blockers to cut the defender, because the sprint-out goes so fast that they could never hope to recover in time to stop the play. The idea of area blocking by the onside linemen will also negate any attempt made by the defense to blitz or penetrate towards the side of the sprint-out. In the diagrams that follow, onside blocking is shown as it may accommodate several different defensive tactics. (See Diagrams 7-1 through 7-3.)

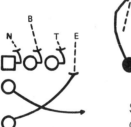

DIAGRAM 7-1

Sprint-out right vs. 52 defense with blitz by onside linebacker.

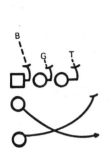

DIAGRAM 7-2

Sprint-out right vs. 44 defense with onside line-backer blitz.

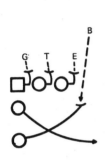

DIAGRAM 7-3

Sprint-out right vs. gap 8 defense and outside blitz.

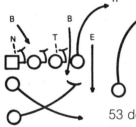

DIAGRAM 7-4

53 defense with double blitzing puts great pressure on the passer.

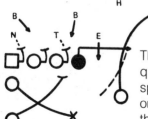

DIAGRAM 7-5

The offense adjusts the tight end's pattern for quick pass in flat. The passer may also adjust his sprint-out and set up to throw rather than throw on the run. Line and fullback blocking remains the same.

The sprint-out pass requires an aggressive block at the corner as indicated by the block of the fullback in the above diagrams. This block may be accomplished in many ways, but the most effective block is the threat of a running play. No fake between quarterback and fullback is necessary as long as there is some sort of running play established with this play-action. Although the onside linemen take a position step to the same side of the sprint-out, they are limited in their assignment to block only the defender on their outside shoulder. If a defender lines up on the tight end, for example, the onside tackle is not responsible for blocking that far to the outside. He will simply take his position steps and block the area head-on him and to his inside. The blocker who is responsible for the corner, in this case the fullback, is assigned to block the first man to appear outside his onside tackle. If more than one defender crosses the outside corner in an effort to put more pressure on the passer, then the sprint-out may be altered or a quick receiver may be added, both of which have the effect of forcing the defense to drop one man off for pass defense. Diagram 7-4 shows a defensive move to stop the sprint-out to the tight end side, while Diagram 7-5 shows how the offense would counteract this without changing the offensive line rules.

If an extra blocker were needed at the onside corner, a man in motion would be brought over and in some cases be used as a blocker or as a third receiver to flood the zones.

Backside Blocking

The backside refers to that part of the interior line away from the direction of the sprint-out. If the sprint-out goes right, then the left guard and left tackle are termed backside. The blocking techniques of the backside are different, for defenders attacking from this side are approaching the passer unseen by him, and more time is required to block these pass rushers. The technique for the backside linemen is simply the cup type of drop-back protection outlined in Chapter 6. Remember that cup protection is also area-type blocking and should account for blitzing as well as regular defensive tactics. The backside linemen will still take their initial jab step toward the side of the sprint-out, but unlike the onside linemen, their second step is a drop step on a 45-degree angle with the line of scrimmage. Once this position is taken, the backside blockers will protect their inside area first and from there, they will block any defender coming head-on them or slightly to their outside. If more than two defenders put the rush on from the backside area, the outermost rushers will go unblocked, for they are entirely too far away from the passer to make the play. Diagrams 7-6 through 7-8 show several defenses and how the backside linemen would pick them up.

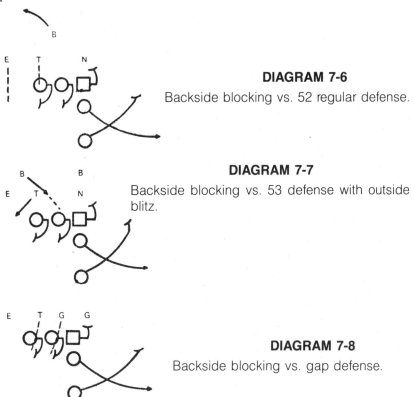

DIAGRAM 7-6

Backside blocking vs. 52 regular defense.

DIAGRAM 7-7

Backside blocking vs. 53 defense with outside blitz.

DIAGRAM 7-8

Backside blocking vs. gap defense.

The backside linemen may use any one of the three types of drop-back pass protection techniques to block on the sprint-out. Backside blocking using these techniques is less dangerous than drop-back passing, because the passer's pocket gets further away with each second the rusher is delayed. For this reason, a lineman does not have to be a great pass blocker as long as he has been taught enough ways to stop or slow down the charging lineman coming from the backside. Again, the act of hitting, retreating, and finally cutting the defender makes for very effective pass protection on the backside of the sprint-out. Diagrams 7-9 and 7-10 depict several ways that the backside linemen may block for the sprint-out passer.

The basics of blocking for any pass, whether it is a drop-back pass, a sprint-out pass, or any form of pass, should never change. Balance, position and foot-fire are always vital to effective pass blocking.

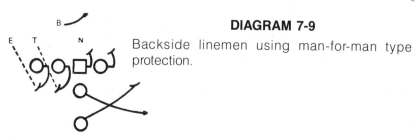

DIAGRAM 7-9

Backside linemen using man-for-man type protection.

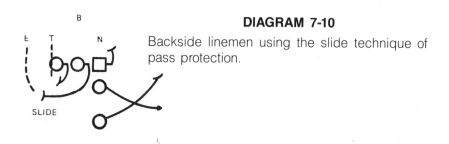

DIAGRAM 7-10

Backside linemen using the slide technique of pass protection.

VARIATIONS IN SPRINT-OUT BLOCKING

The blocking patterns offered above are the simplest ways to block effectively for the sprint-out pass, but this does not imply that they are the only ways. There are a multitude of blocking schemes that will accommodate your sprint-out pass as well as your running game, and we will demonstrate several of these more sophisticated blocking schemes in this section. In many cases, the major change is centered around the blocking of the defender who attacks the quarterback at the corner. As previously indicated, this defender may be blocked by one or more of the offensive backs. However, it is also a popular maneuver to block the corner with a pulling guard. In Diagram 7-11, the onside guard pulls to block the defensive end. The onside tackle and end block down to stop penetration and the fullback slants through the opening and flares into the short flat zone. A perfect complement to this pass play is the short trap diagrammed in 7-12.

The backside linemen are, of course, still able to block according to regular drop-back techniques. There would be no change for them in a situation like this. However, it is also possible to block the backside differently and disguise the sprint-out pass with another sound running play. Diagram 7-13 shows how the common sweep play, with its two pulling linemen, can be alerted to fit a sprint-out philosophy. Diagram 7-14 maps out the blocking patterns for the line that will give the defensive secondary false keys and add to the surprise of the sprint-out pass.

No matter how you decide to vary the pattern of blocking for the sprint-out game, several things must always be considered to be of the prime importance:

1. Block the sprint-out corner as strongly as possible.

2. Use any type of blocking consistent with your philosophy on passing. Do not burden your blockers with a multitude of techniques.

3. Protect the inside lines of pursuit to the quarterback primarily; then worry about the outside lines.

4. When the sprint-out pass is defended or stopped, adjust patterns or style of sprint-out; do not adjust or change interior line rules.

5. Use a variety of sprint-out blocking patterns to confuse secondary and defenders at the corner.

6. Use the sprint-out series to run, throw short, throw deep, run reverse and/or counters, screens and draws.

One particular series from our own sprint-out game is offered here as an example of item #6. In this series we were able to do a variety of things that no opponent ever stopped completely. (See Diagrams 7-15 through 7-22.)

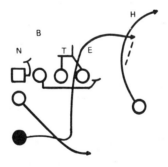

DIAGRAM 7-11

Onside guard blocks at the corner while tight end and tackle block solidly. The fullback flares in short flat.

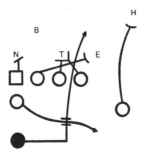

DIAGRAM 7-12

A perfect complement to the sprint-out series would be this short trap off-tackle with fullback carrying.

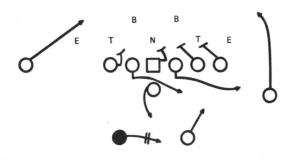

**DIAGRAM 7-13:
THE SWEEP PLAY.**

Both guards lead the play, quarterback rolls into sprint-out route.

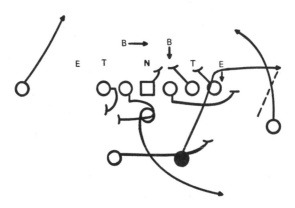

DIAGRAM 7-14: THE SWEEP ACTION SPRINT-OUT PASS.

Lead guard blocks the corner, and trail guard peels back to protect the backside.

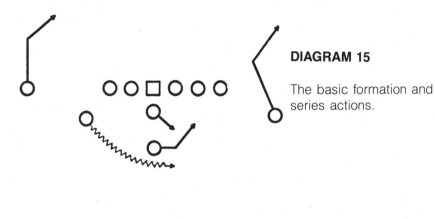

DIAGRAM 15

The basic formation and series actions.

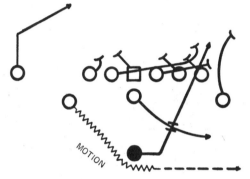

DIAGRAM 7-16

Fullback power sweep with motion.

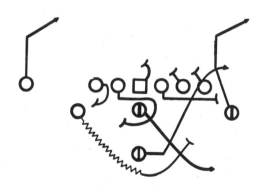

DIAGRAM 7-17

Sprint-out right; quarterback has a run/pass option. The motion back helps guard block at the corner.

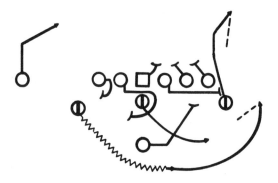

DIAGRAM 7-18

Sprint-out right, with fullback and motion back switching assignments. Run/pass option again for the quarterback.

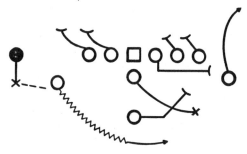

DIAGRAM 7-19

Sprint-out right with quick screen throwback. Quarterback must set before throwing.

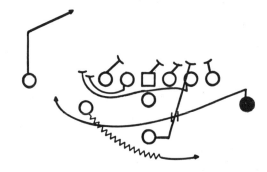

DIAGRAM 7-20

Sprint-out right, wingback reverse. May also be run inside as a draw or trap. Good against teams that shift with motion.

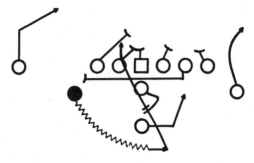

DIAGRAM 7-21

Sprint-out right, counter-trap to slot back in motion. Very effective against teams that shift with motion.

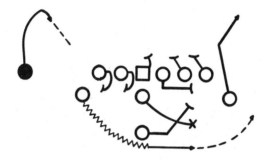

DIAGRAM 7-22

Sprint-out right, throw-back to the split end. This receiver will simply find the open area and come back to the ball.

To make this series even more effective, we can put the wing in motion and run the sprint-out series to the split end's side. Greater variations can be added if the defense does not put great pressure on the corner and you can block that area with only one blocker. If this is possible, then patterns with as many as five receivers are available. Any defense that can stop all the options of the sprint-out series will truly be a well-prepared and well-disciplined opponent, and extremely difficult to beat.

CHAPTER 8

Play-Action Pass Blocking

The play-action pass is the third and final type of pass that we will discuss in this section on the passing game. Its position in this part of the book does not reflect its importance. Quite the contrary; play-action passes are often the heart and soul of the passing attacks of many high school and college football teams, and they are dangerously effective weapons for a team with any kind of a running game. The play-action pass can be used for deception as a change-up for a powerful running attack, or it may be used as a surprise attack after a sudden turnover. More often than not, play-action passes are thrown under twelve yards in depth, and when they are kept short, the percentage of completion increases, making them an effective ball-control weapon. The play-action pass is also excellent for the team with less than average-sized linemen or teams with a less then average throwing quarterback. Because of the necessity of backfield faking, the play-action pass is not conducive to use in a two-minute drill, the way the drop-back and sprint-out passes are. However, the multiplicity of play-action passes far surpasses either of the other two forms of the passing game. Once the blocking skills for the running game and the drop-back passing game have been taught, pass blocking for play-action passes becomes second nature.

A PASSING PHILOSOPHY

We must have reasons for whatever we do, for the heart of successful coaching is preparation, to meet opportunity, not luck. It is therefore proper to state reasons why the play-action pass should be incorporated into your offensive passing attack. The list is endless, but several reasons stand out and are worth explaining:

1. *As a complement to the running game.* If your offense is effective on the ground, averaging three or more yards per play, then chances are

very good that a pass off the same type of play-action will also be successful. In this instance the defense has been drawn in closer by a repetition of successful running plays, amounting to a wide open secondary.

2. *For the benefit of inferior personnel.* If your quarterback is not too tall and can not throw very deep; if your line is relatively small and not too strong; and, if your receivers are not too fast and even a little short, you will never be able to throw a successful drop-back pass. The play-action pass provides great blocking angles for the line, gives the quarterback wide open zones, and the receivers are usually wide open on short patterns. The quality of your athletes should determine whether or not you use this type of pass, but some play-action passes should be used by all teams at one time or another. The innate talents of your ball players will determine just how much you use play-action passes.

3. *To pass on first downs.* If you have a successful running game, why not throw from play-action on first downs? We try to anticipate the defense's train of thought, and whenever possible, unload with the unexpected.

4. *To surprise the defense after a sudden turn-over.* You have just recovered your opponent's fumble inside his own thirty-yard line. He expects a run on first down, the game is a hard fought tie; what do you call? In our opinion, a play-action pass with two receivers, one deep and one short, would be excellent. The defense is probably very dejected over its mistake and will not be alert for the unexpected. Furthermore, should you fail to complete the pass, and even if it gets intercepted, the opponent will not have gained much and you have the possibility of a quick score.

In the long run, play-action passes help reduce the amount of coaching that must go into the season's preparation, for any number of plays may be taught, and then without much extra coaching, the same plays can be turned into passes. The line will simply have to be taught the proper ways to block for play-action passes.

THE STANCE

Since we want the defense to think "run," we must show them every offensive sign we can that a run is coming. To this end we have the cadence, formation and stance on every play-action pass accommodate this philosophy. We don't feel that an offensive blocker can get a good charge from a two-point stance for the running game, so, unlike the drop-back and the sprint-out pass, we would never start a play-action pass from the quick count or the pre-set stance. Every play-action pass will start from the perfect three-point stance, or whichever stance is considered the normal set position in your offense. As indicated earlier, we never retreat in play-action passes, therefore, a well-balanced, three-point stance is a must for the more aggressive blocking that benefits play-action passes.

DISGUISING THE PLAY-ACTION PASS

As the name implies, this type of pass is disguised by the action of the backfield. The backs will go through their normal routes for the makings of a particular running play. Since many younger players habitually key the running backs, this makes for a very effective disguise. Even more effective is the use of two or more wide receivers or motion backs when running play-action passes. These particular extras added to the color of the pass play force the defensive backs to focus their attention even more so on the backs or on the wide receivers, or even on the man in motion. This point is illustrated in the following diagrams where a number of offensive sets are used to run the same play-action pass. (See Diagrams 8-1 through 8-3.)

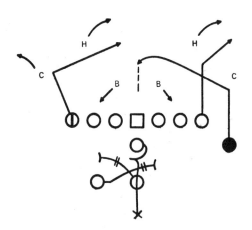

DIAGRAM 8-1

Scissors action-pass that delays the linebackers' pass defense and leaves the middle zone area free. A secondary receiver may be sent deeper.

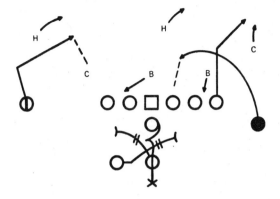

DIAGRAM 8-2

The same backfield action with the added attraction of two wide receivers. The secondary must spread itself out more and still try to react to the running play. This makes open lanes greater and allows more time for deeper patterns.

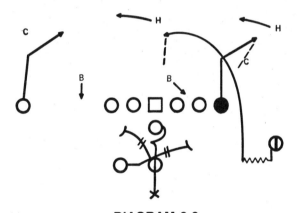

DIAGRAM 8-3

The same backfield action with a man-in-motion. This technique forces the defense to rotate out of position while the receivers find the vacated areas.

So far the disguises we have described pertain to the backfield action, but these disguises can be lost if the offensive line doesn't disguise its blocking techniques also. A simple comparison will prove my point. In the drop-back pass, the blockers must set up and drop-step to get a sound blocking position on the pass rusher. Furthermore, since the rules forbid interior linemen to go past the line of scrimmage on passes, the secondary can key on the line's footwork and read that a pass is coming almost immediately. The sprint-out pass takes a little more pressure off the offense and makes key-reading more difficult, but since some of the blockers have to drop back to protect the passer, again the disguise is incomplete. On the other hand, play-action passes are not only characterized by backfield faking, but the initial move of every lineman reflects the same move they would make if the play were a run. Consequently, if the defensive secondary is geared to key only the backfield, or only the offensive line, they will be in deep trouble trying to stop play-action passes. This initial movement by the blockers is not vital to the success of the overall block, but it is vital to the disguise of the play-action pass.

THE INITIAL STEP

The initial step in play-action pass blocking boils down to an aggressive step similar to the step taken in blocking for the actual running play. To accommodate the rules that go along with the passing game, the linemen must avoid going downfield during the play, and this calls for special techniques that will be described shortly. The initial step can best be controlled by the blocking rules that go along with running plays with slight variations. Consider the following example: the blocking rules for the running game are given as priorities. That is, for all plays, the blocking rules for interior linemen are:

(1.) Block inside gap first.
(2.) Block man head-on second.
(3.) Block outside gap third.

Use these same rules for blocking play-action passes and the correct initial steps will follow. The priority rules listed above are diagrammed for a particular play-action pass in 8-4. Note how the initial steps of the pass blocking unit resemble run-action. This technique helps disguise the play.

Some highly successful offenses, such as the triple option with bone offense, and the twin veer offense, predicate their play-action passes on the same blocking rules as the running game. In this way, the teaching of extra techniques is kept at a minimum while deception is kept at a maximum. Thus, whatever your blocking rules tell your

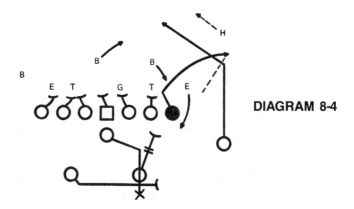

DIAGRAM 8-4

linemen to do on running plays should also guide them in their initial steps on play-action pass blocking. The pairs of diagrams that follow show simple running plays coupled with an effective play-action pass, both of which show the same initial steps taken by the interior linemen. (See Diagrams 8-5 through 8-8.)

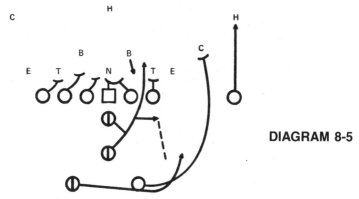

DIAGRAM 8-5

The triple option from the wishbone formation.

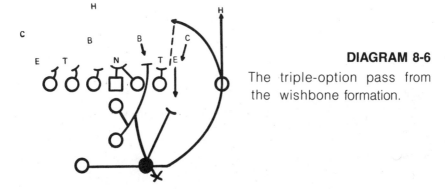

DIAGRAM 8-6

The triple-option pass from the wishbone formation.

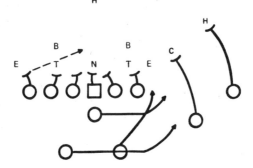

DIAGRAM 8-7

The triple option from the twin veer setup.

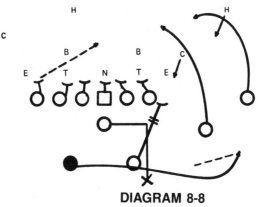

DIAGRAM 8-8

The swing or screen pass from triple-option action.

AGGRESSIVE BLOCKING

There are a great many coaching books about the passing game, and when we refer to play-action passes and the blocking that goes with it, we will always advocate aggressive blocking. What is aggressive blocking? Isn't all blocking supposed to be aggressive? Clarification is needed in an effort to understand this term. What writers are trying to distinguish is the difference between drop-back pass blocking, which allows the pass rusher to come to the blocker, and play-action pass blocking which requires the blocker to attack the defender. We don't want our players to think that aggressive blocking is only a part of play-action passes, but we do want them to know the different techniques required in various passing styles. The blocker must understand that his job in play-action pass protection is not only to prevent the defender from getting to the passer, but also to make the pass look like a run. To that end he must fire-out on the snap and attack the defender with 100% aggressiveness, never for a moment fearing that his aggressiveness will make him an ineligible receiver.

THE PROPER BLOCK

We have laid the foundation for a successful play-action pass:

1. The philosophy and reasoning are sound.
2. The disguises are built into the offense.
3. The blocking rules are consistent with the running game.

Now all that is left is a simple, consistent technique that will allow the blocker to be aggressive without the fear of crossing the neutral zone and becoming ineligible. Our advice is to use a block that will permit the blocker to make solid contact that can be maintained for several seconds and that will enable the blocker to turn the defender laterally down the line of scrimmage so that he can execute his block without ever crossing the line of scrimmage. We therefore teach all our offensive linemen the techniques of the following blocks used in one-on-one blocking (refer to Chapter 1 for full details):

1. *The drive block.* As described in Chapter 1, the drive block demands that the blocker get a quick start off the line, that he make good initial contact, that he accelerate on contact with the defender, and that he turn the defender away from the action laterally down the line. This type of block is especially good when the defender is in a head-on position.

2. *The cartwheel block.* The blocker may well use this technique to show the aggressive attitude necessary to fool the defense, but at the same time, no forward driving is required. Once good contact is made as in the initial phase of a scramble block, the blocker will cartwheel his hips 180 degrees around the defender to prevent him from pursuit. An excellent follow-through for the cartwheel block is the technique called "crabbing" that helps the blocker move the defender laterally down the line.

3. *The hook block.* Defenders who align on the outside gap or outside shoulder of the blocker may pose a slight problem unless the techniques of hook blocking are perfected. In reality, the hook block only requires a quick jab-step for position, and then it becomes nothing more than a scramble block or a cartwheel block depending upon how contact is maintained.

Regardless of the blocking technique used, the fundamentals of stance, initial step, balance, foot-fire, and technique must always be perfect. These three blocking types will provide these advantages for your linemen when blocking for the play-action pass:

1. An aggressive attack at the defender.
2. Maximum contact surface.
3. Low position on the defender to prevent him from raising his hands and blocking the pass.
4. The ability to block for several seconds without crossing the neutral zone.
5. Disguising the pass to slow down pass rush and secondary's reaction.

UNCOVERED LINEMEN

The uncovered lineman can not go after a linebacker the way he would for a running play. However, the fact that he does not have a defender on or near him does not eliminate him from using any of the play-action pass blocking techniques just described. He must still fire-out quickly in a low position and attack the unmanned area closest to the normal blocking area he would be responsible for on a running play. He makes this move to continue the disguise of the play and as an anticipation of a slant or blitz that may come into this uncovered area. The typical example of such a case is against the stacked or tandem defense. In the situation diagrammed in 8-9, the right guard must anticipate that the middle linebacker and the nose-guard will be dealing, and therefore, he attacks the area the same way he would for the running game. If the stunt does materialize, the guard is ready; if not, then he will help the nearest lineman in a two-on-one situation. (See Diagram 8-9.)

PULLING LINEMEN

Some of the best plays in football are off-tackle power plays, traps, and sweeps. A common characteristic of these types of plays is that a lineman is pulled out of the line and assigned to block at the point of attack so that the offensive blockers will outnumber the defenders. If a team is successful running these types of plays, the defense will soon begin keying solely on these pulling linemen. When this happens, the offensive team can throw a play-action pass from the fake power, or the fake trap, or the fake sweep. But, in order for this type of pass to be devastating, the interior linemen must still execute their pulling blocks. It is perfectly suitable for play-action pass blocking to pull a lineman out of the line and have him block just as he would for the running play, because in power blocks, or traps, or sweeps, the lineman can show aggressiveness, make good contact, and still avoid crossing the neutral zone. Once the pulling lineman gets to the point of attack, he may use either the scramble block, the cartwheel block, or the hook block, judging from how the initial contact is made. If it happens that the defender does not penetrate, then the pulling blocker will simply pass block at the assigned area the same way he would for drop-back or sprint-out protection. It is imperative, of course, that the backfield action remain the same and that the other blockers show aggressiveness and continue to block according to their rules for the running game. Diagrams 8-10 through 8-15 depict several very successful running plays and their complementary passes. The general flow of the blocking linemen gives the defense the impression of "run" while the receivers are able to get open in their pass routes. Often, plays of this nature result in big gainers after the ball is caught.

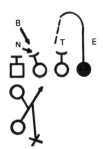

DIAGRAM 8-9

Right guard's step vs. 53 stack on play-action pass protection.

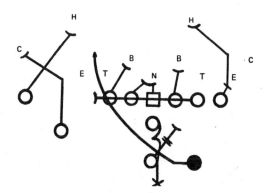

DIAGRAM 8-10

Scissors play with trapping action.

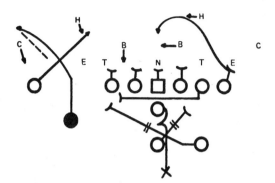

DIAGRAM 8-11

Scissors pass with same trapping action.

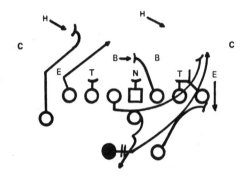

DIAGRAM 8-12

Typical power play off tackle.

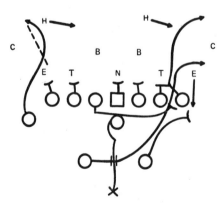

DIAGRAM 8-13

Same power play action for play-action pass.

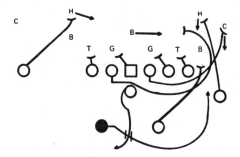

DIAGRAM 8-14

The pro sweep.

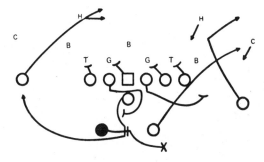

DIAGRAM 8-15

The pro sweep, with halfback option pass.